# STAR WARS®

## THE CLONE WARS™
### EPISODE GUIDE

WRITTEN BY
**JASON FRY**

# CONTENTS

# HOW TO USE THIS BOOK

*Star Wars: The Clone Wars Episode Guide* brings together every episode of seasons one through five of the hit television series, presented as never before. Here you'll find the episodes in the order of the Clone Wars storyline, rather than in the order they were written and broadcast. Above are the episode names so you can find your favorites, and there is also an icon that indicates which season they belong to. Every episode is explored in a double-page spread, with story highlights, in-depth facts, and panels showing the key characters, vehicles, droids, and locations. A data file also gives each episode a number referring to its position in the storyline, along with its episode and season number, original US airdate, director, and writer.

# INTRODUCTION

## A long time ago in a galaxy far, far away....

The Clone Wars have engulfed the galaxy! Billions of battle droids have invaded the Republic, built by greedy corporations and commanded by their Separatist masters: the charismatic leader Count Dooku, cyborg warlord General Grievous, and the mysterious Darth Sidious.

Opposing the Separatists' vast armies are clone troopers, created to serve and defend the Republic with unquestioning loyalty to its embattled leader, Supreme Chancellor Palpatine. Thousands of Jedi Knights have agreed to lead the clones as the Republic's generals, abandoning their traditional role of peacekeepers during the galaxy's hour of need.

The mightiest of the Jedi is Anakin Skywalker, rumored to be the Chosen One destined to bring balance to the Force. Anakin often fights alongside his former master, Obi-Wan Kenobi, and his Padawan: the bold, sometimes brash Ahsoka Tano. But Anakin has a secret. He has violated the rules of the Jedi Order by marrying Padmé Amidala. Padmé is the outspoken senator from the planet Naboo, who seeks to use her role to bring an end to the war.

Anakin and Obi-Wan have allies in their fight: Yoda and Mace Windu, the heads of the Jedi Order; the droids C-3PO and R2-D2; and brave clone soldiers, such as Captain Rex. Their adventures bring them alongside friends and foes: the peace-seeking Duchess Satine of Mandalore; the ruthless bounty hunter Cad Bane; and the devious pirate Hondo Ohnaka. As the Clone Wars entangle more and more planets, the fate of the galaxy and a thousand generations of civilization hang in the balance....

# A SEPARATIST TASK FORCE

commanded by the legendary Admiral Trench is blockading the planet Christophsis. After Anakin Skywalker fails to break through Trench's lines, Obi-Wan Kenobi arrives with an experimental stealth ship. Its cloaking device renders it invisible and enables Anakin and veteran officer Admiral Yularen to play a dangerous game of cat-and-mouse with the crafty Trench.

## FOLLOWING ORDERS
Obi-Wan says that the stealth ship will enable Anakin to slip through the blockade and deliver supplies to Senator Bail Organa, who is trapped on Christophsis. But Anakin has a more important task in mind—outwitting Trench.

# CAT AND MOUSE

"A WISE LEADER KNOWS WHEN TO FOLLOW."

### NOTABLE CHARACTERS

**Anakin Skywalker**

**Admiral Yularen**

**Admiral Trench**

### VEHICLES

**Jedi Cruiser**

**Separatist Dreadnought**

**Stealth Ship**

### LOCATION

**Christophsis**

### DROID

**Tactical Droid**

Trench doesn't mind using unskilled battle droids as pilots: A true strategist outthinks his opponent and so never has to outfly him.

| #1 EPISODE 16, SEASON 2 | AIRDATE MARCH 26, 2010 | DIRECTOR KYLE DUNLEVY | WRITER BRIAN LARSEN |

**A CHANGE OF TACTICS**
While taunting the Jedi, Trench reveals that he has faced a cloaked ship before. Anakin and Yularen examine the tactics Trench used in such situations to find a pattern they can exploit.

**ANAKIN'S GAMBLE**
When Trench lowers his shields to fire torpedoes at Anakin, the Jedi steers his stealth ship toward Trench's bridge. The torpedoes follow Anakin's path and hit Trench's own ship instead!

**A CHANGE OF NAME**
The spider-like Admiral Trench was originally named Admiral Taranch. This spelling can be seen (in Aurebesh) on Yularen's intelligence report.

**CLOAKING DEVICES**
In Episode V: *The Empire Strikes Back*, Captain Needa insists that no ship as small as the *Millennium Falcon* could have a cloaking device.

Trench regards war as a great game and enjoys matching wits with a worthy opponent such as Anakin Skywalker.

**"I smell FEAR ... and it smells GOOD."**

ADMIRAL TRENCH

## AFTER BARELY ESCAPING

a Separatist ambush on Christophsis, Jedi Knight Anakin and Obi-Wan realize a traitor is leaking the Republic's plans to their enemies. Commander Cody and Captain Rex investigate and come to the disturbing realization that the traitor is one of their fellow clone troopers. How do they outthink an adversary who is identical to them?

### TRAITOR IN THE RANKS

The clones fight the Separatist battle droids for the strategically located planet of Christophsis. Everywhere they go, it seems as though the enemy is one step ahead.

# THE HIDDEN ENEMY

## "TRUTH ENLIGHTENS THE MIND, BUT WON'T ALWAYS BRING HAPPINESS TO YOUR HEART."

**NOTABLE CHARACTERS**

Captain Rex

Commander Cody

Sergeant Slick

Cody finds the comlink built into clone troopers' helmets unreliable, so uses a longer-range communications unit built into his armor.

| #2 EPISODE 16, SEASON 1 | AIRDATE FEBRUARY 6, 2009 | DIRECTOR STEWARD LEE | WRITER DREW Z. GREENBE |
|---|---|---|---|

## VENTRESS AWAITS
Despite suspecting there is a spy in their midst, Obi-Wan and Anakin decide to search behind Separatist lines to get answers. They run into Asajj Ventress, who is in a fighting mood.

## CLONE AGAINST CLONE
Cody and Rex discover the traitor is Sergeant Slick, a fellow trooper who thinks the Republic has enslaved its army of clones. They must stop Slick and lock him up before he does any more damage to their defenses.

### DROIDS

**Battle Droid**

**Super Battle Droid**

**Octuptarra Droid**

Rex's armor bears the blue markings of the 501st Legion. Rex leads Torrent Company alongside Anakin Skywalker.

### COMIC ORIGINS
Rex was originally named Alpha, an ARC trooper introduced in the *Star Wars: Republic* series by Dark Horse Comics.

# "It's the JEDI that keep my brothers ENSLAVED."
SERGEANT SLICK

## THE CLONE WARS

**ON CHRISTOPHSIS**, Jedi Knight Anakin Skywalker meets Ahsoka Tano, his new Padawan. After defeating a Separatist attack, the two are sent to find Jabba the Hutt's kidnapped son, Rotta. Anakin and Ahsoka are stumbling into a trap. Count Dooku and Ziro the Hutt plan to frame the Jedi for the kidnapping in order to shift the Hutts' allegiance from the Republic to the Separatists.

### INTO BATTLE
Clones and battle droids face off on the strategically located planet of Christophsis. Anakin and Obi-Wan support their troops in a desperate fight against Count Dooku's legions.

### NOTABLE CHARACTERS

**Anakin Skywalker**

**Ahsoka Tano**

**Obi-Wan Kenobi**

**Padmé Amidala**

### VEHICLES

**Assault Gunship**

**AV-7 Cannon**

### THE BIG SCREEN
The theatrical release was created from what was originally intended to be the first three episodes of the television series, plus an introduction to Ahsoka on Christophsis.

**THEATRICAL RELEASE**

**AIRDATE**
AUGUST 15, 2008

**DIRECTOR**
DAVE FILONI

**WRITERS**
HENRY GILROY, STEVEN MELCHING, AND SCOTT MURPH

THE STORY CONTINUES ...

## THE NEW PADAWAN
Yoda has sent Ahsoka Tano to Christophsis to serve as Anakin's Padawan. She helps turn the tide in the battle and then heads for the planet Teth with Anakin to rescue Rotta the Huttlet.

## TOUGH CLIMB
On Teth, Captain Rex's clones face a daunting task: to scale a vertical cliff and attack a palace full of battle droids. Anakin and Ahsoka lead the clones on this perilous mission.

Anakin never wanted a Padawan, convinced an apprentice would only slow him down. But Yoda hopes the responsibility of being a teacher will help Anakin learn how to let go of his dangerous emotional attachments.

### FAMILIAR VOICES
For the theatrical release, Samuel L. Jackson (Mace Windu), Christopher Lee (Count Dooku), Anthony Daniels (C-3PO), and Matthew Wood reprise their prequel trilogy roles. Daniels and Wood would go on to do the television series.

## DROIDS

| LEP Servant Droid | LR-57 Combat Droid | FA-4 Pilot Droid |

## "READY he is, to TEACH an apprentice. To let go of his pupil, a greater CHALLENGE it will be."

YODA

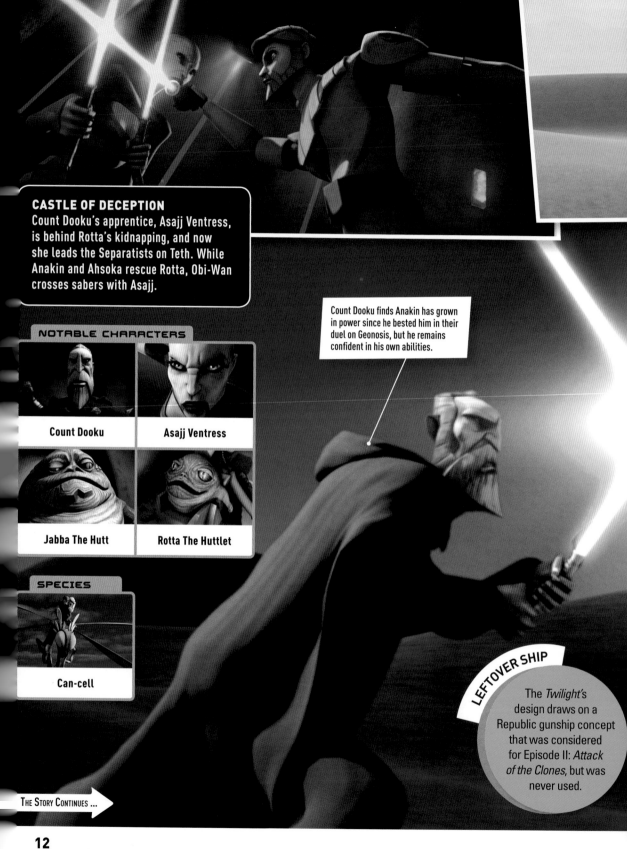

### CASTLE OF DECEPTION

Count Dooku's apprentice, Asajj Ventress, is behind Rotta's kidnapping, and now she leads the Separatists on Teth. While Anakin and Ahsoka rescue Rotta, Obi-Wan crosses sabers with Asajj.

Count Dooku finds Anakin has grown in power since he bested him in their duel on Geonosis, but he remains confident in his own abilities.

#### NOTABLE CHARACTERS

**Count Dooku**

**Asajj Ventress**

**Jabba The Hutt**

**Rotta The Huttlet**

#### SPECIES

**Can-cell**

#### LEFTOVER SHIP

The *Twilight's* design draws on a Republic gunship concept that was considered for Episode II: *Attack of the Clones*, but was never used.

THE STORY CONTINUES ...

## UNHAPPY HOMECOMING
After crash-landing the freighter *Twilight* on Tatooine, Anakin and Ahsoka make their way to Jabba's palace to return Rotta. But they do not guess that they are walking into a trap: Count Dooku awaits them.

## THE PLOT IS REVEALED
While Anakin duels Dooku on Tatooine, Padmé Amidala discovers that Ziro the Hutt plotted the kidnapping with Dooku. When clone troopers capture Ziro, he admits his role in the plot. Dooku's plans are ruined!

Anakin grew up on Tatooine, and returning to his homeworld reminds him of his mother's death, stirring dark feelings in him.

### VEHICLE

*Twilight*

### LOCATIONS

Teth

Tatooine

**ON KAMINO**, Domino Squad, made up of five clone cadets—Echo, Fives, Hevy, Droidbait, and Cutup—struggle to complete the training exercises necessary for graduation. Jedi Master Shaak Ti oversees their training and faces a hard decision: If the feuding clones of Domino Squad don't learn to work together quickly, she will have to reject them as unfit for military duty.

## FALLEN DOMINOS

In training exercises on Kamino, the Dominos usually fail because they bicker and think only of themselves. They are in danger of being removed from the cadet program.

# CLONE CADETS

### "BROTHERS IN ARMS ARE BROTHERS FOR LIFE."

**THX 1138**

Commander Colt, who also oversees the clones' training, orders a challenge called "version THX, variable 11–38"—a reference to George Lucas's first feature film, *THX 1138*.

**VEHICLE**

Republic Assault Ship

**LOCATION**

Kamino

### NOTABLE CHARACTERS

Hevy

Bric

99

**#3**
EPISODE 1, SEASON 3

**AIRDATE**
SEPTEMBER 17, 2010

**DIRECTOR**
DAVE FILONI

**WRITER**
CAMERON LITVACK

14

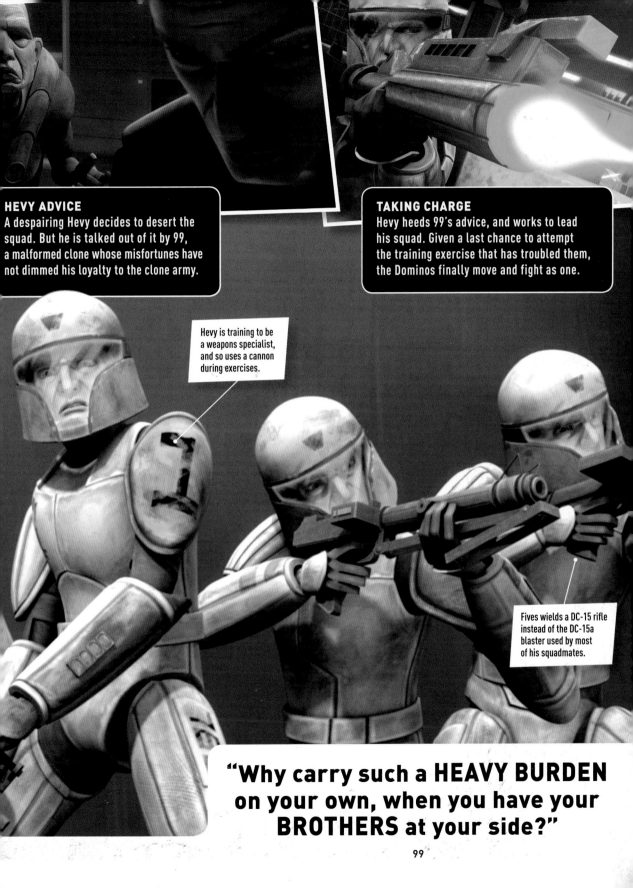

**HEVY ADVICE**
A despairing Hevy decides to desert the squad. But he is talked out of it by 99, a malformed clone whose misfortunes have not dimmed his loyalty to the clone army.

**TAKING CHARGE**
Hevy heeds 99's advice, and works to lead his squad. Given a last chance to attempt the training exercise that has troubled them, the Dominos finally move and fight as one.

Hevy is training to be a weapons specialist, and so uses a cannon during exercises.

Fives wields a DC-15 rifle instead of the DC-15a blaster used by most of his squadmates.

"Why carry such a HEAVY BURDEN on your own, when you have your BROTHERS at your side?"

**THE SEPARATISTS** have blockaded Ryloth and invaded the Twi'lek planet, endangering freedom fighter Cham Syndulla and Jedi Master Ima-Gun Di. Senator Bail Organa and Jar Jar Binks ask Toydaria's King Katuunko for help, but he needs his world to appear neutral while the Separatists are watching. The king agrees to help, however, if the Republic vistors can keep his involvement a secret.

### THE KING'S DILEMMA
King Katuunko feels powerless. He wants to help the Republic relieve the siege of Ryloth, but cannot risk the Separatists' wrath if he is caught taking sides in the war.

Battle droid commanders can be distinguished from other droids by their yellow markings.

## SUPPLY LINES
### "WHERE THERE'S A WILL, THERE'S A WAY."

**WHAT'S IN A NAME?**

The name of Jedi Master Ima-Gun Di gives a not-so-subtle hint about his fate ("I'm gonna die").

| | #4<br>EPISODE 3, SEASON 3 | AIRDATE<br>SEPTEMBER 24, 2010 | DIRECTOR<br>BRIAN KALIN<br>O'CONNELL | WRITERS<br>STEVEN MELCHIN<br>AND EOGHAN MAHO |
|---|---|---|---|---|

## JAR JAR BINKS LENDS A HAND

Katuunko says Organa can use Toydaria to transfer supplies to ships bound for Ryloth—but only if the Separatists don't find out. They organize a banquet to distract the Separatist Lott Dodd, and Jar Jar provides the entertainment, juggling plates while the supplies are being transferred.

## DI AND KEELI'S LAST STAND

Meanwhile, Ima-Gun Di blows up a gunship and blocks a strategic mountain pass, giving Syndulla's fighters time to escape the Separatist forces. Di and Captain Keeli hold off the battle droids as best they can, but Di does not survive.

### NOTABLE CHARACTERS

**Jar Jar Binks**

**Senator Bail Organa**

**King Katuunko**

### LOCATIONS

**Tantive**

**Toydaria**

### SPECIES

**Blurrg**

This Republic gunship is packed with enough explosives to seal off the mountain pass.

## "For the REPUBLIC! For the TWI'LEKS!"

MASTER DI

**YODA TRAVELS** to the coral moon of Rugosa to convince Toydaria's King Katuunko to assist the Republic, but Asajj Ventress also seeks the king's allegiance. After Yoda's ship is shot down, he proposes a wager: He and his clone troopers will battle Ventress's droid army to demonstrate which side is more resourceful.

## VENTRESS ON A MISSION
After learning that the Republic plans to meet with Toydaria's King Katuunko, Count Dooku arranges an ambush of Yoda's starship and sends Ventress to secure the king's loyalties.

The cannons of the Separatists' AATs aren't powerful enough to blast through Rugosa's petrified coral forests.

### VERSATILE VOICE
Voice actor Tom Kane provides the voice for Yoda and Admiral Yularen. He also narrates the opening of each episode.

## AMBUSH

## "GREAT LEADERS INSPIRE GREATNESS IN OTHERS."

### NOTABLE CHARACTERS

**Yoda**

**King Katuunko**

**Asajj Ventress**

**#5**
EPISODE 1, SEASON 1

**AIRDATE**
OCTOBER 3, 2008

**DIRECTOR**
DAVE BULLOCK

**WRITER**
STEVEN MELCHING

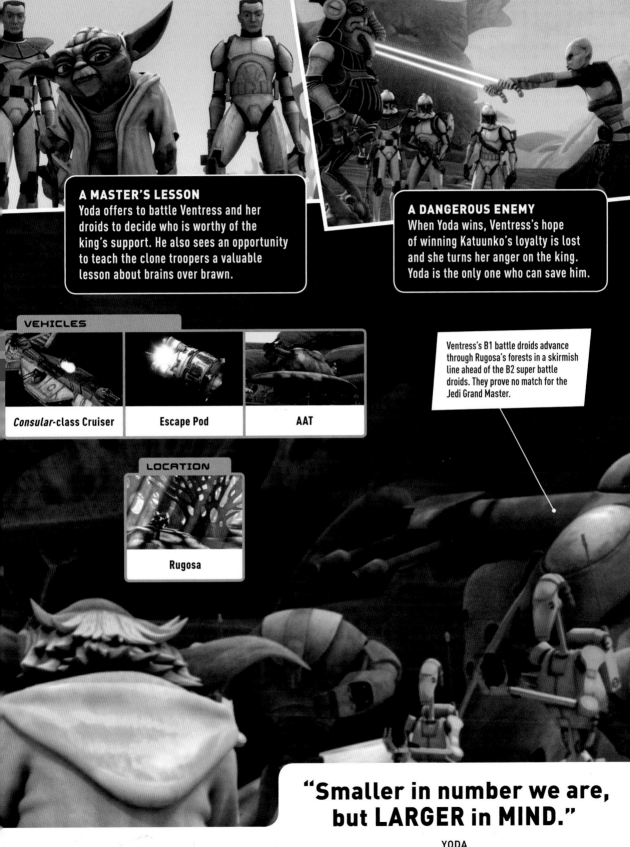

### A MASTER'S LESSON
Yoda offers to battle Ventress and her droids to decide who is worthy of the king's support. He also sees an opportunity to teach the clone troopers a valuable lesson about brains over brawn.

### A DANGEROUS ENEMY
When Yoda wins, Ventress's hope of winning Katuunko's loyalty is lost and she turns her anger on the king. Yoda is the only one who can save him.

## VEHICLES

| *Consular*-class Cruiser | Escape Pod | AAT |
| --- | --- | --- |

## LOCATION

Rugosa

Ventress's B1 battle droids advance through Rugosa's forests in a skirmish line ahead of the B2 super battle droids. They prove no match for the Jedi Grand Master.

## "Smaller in number we are, but LARGER in MIND."

YODA

**GENERAL GRIEVOUS'S** new warship, the massive *Malevolence*, destroys a Republic task force with its fearsome ion cannons. The ship leaves Jedi Master Plo Koon marooned in space with clone Commander Wolffe and two troopers. As battle droids scour the debris for Master Plo and his men, Anakin and Ahsoka disobey the Jedi Council, who don't want to risk losing more ships, and race off to attempt a rescue.

## LOST IN SPACE
Following the attack on their ship, Plo and his troops face a horrible fate: General Grievous's battle droids are searching the debris for escape pods and ripping them open.

### CANNON POWER
The firing channel of the *Malevolence*'s ion cannon looks like the Death Star superlaser in Episode IV: *A New Hope*.

# RISING MALEVOLENCE

### "BELIEF IS NOT A MATTER OF CHANCE, BUT OF CONVICTION."

The *Twilight* looks like a typically dingy freighter, but her previous owners customized her engines and weapons, making her surprisingly fast and capable. And her pilot, Anakin Skywalker, can fly anything in the galaxy.

### DROID
**Rocket Battle Droid**

### VEHICLES
**Malevolence**

**Droch Boarding Ship**

**#6**
EPISODE 2, SEASON 1

**AIRDATE**
OCTOBER 3, 2008

**DIRECTOR**
DAVE FILONI

**WRITER**
STEVEN MELCH

20

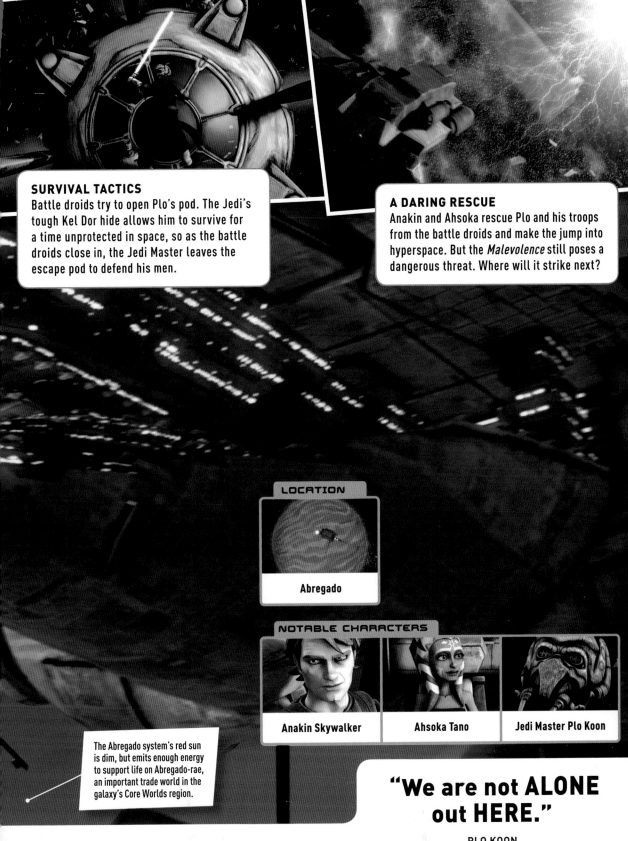

## SURVIVAL TACTICS
Battle droids try to open Plo's pod. The Jedi's tough Kel Dor hide allows him to survive for a time unprotected in space, so as the battle droids close in, the Jedi Master leaves the escape pod to defend his men.

## A DARING RESCUE
Anakin and Ahsoka rescue Plo and his troops from the battle droids and make the jump into hyperspace. But the *Malevolence* still poses a dangerous threat. Where will it strike next?

### LOCATION

**Abregado**

### NOTABLE CHARACTERS

**Anakin Skywalker**

**Ahsoka Tano**

**Jedi Master Plo Koon**

The Abregado system's red sun is dim, but emits enough energy to support life on Abregado-rae, an important trade world in the galaxy's Core Worlds region.

## "We are not ALONE out HERE."

PLO KOON

# SHADOW OF MALEVOLENCE

**GENERAL GRIEVOUS'S** imposing ship, the *Malevolence*, has a new target: a Republic medical station housing thousands of injured clone troopers. The Jedi realize Grievous is about to attack their troops at their most vulnerable, so Anakin leads a fighter squadron through a dangerous nebula to ambush the Separatist dreadnought. But there is no guarantee that the Republic bombers will be able to stop Grievous's ship.

**MISSION BRIEFING**
Anakin Skywalker briefs the clone pilots of Shadow Squadron. He has a daring plan to attack the *Malevolence* and destroy General Grievous.

"EASY IS THE PATH TO WISDOM FOR THOSE NOT BLINDED BY EGO."

**BATTLEWORN SHIPS**
Y-wing fighters take part in the assault on the *Death Star* in Episode IV: *A New Hope*. By then they are considered old ships, valued for being able to take a lot of abuse.

**LOCATION**

Kaliida Nebula

**SPECIES**

Neebray

Having released their payloads of torpedoes, Shadow Squadron's Y-wings race to reach a safe distance from the damaged *Malevolence*.

**#7**
EPISODE 3, SEASON 1

**AIRDATE**
OCTOBER 10, 2008

**DIRECTOR**
BRIAN KALIN O'CONNELL

**WRITER**
STEVEN MELCHING

## BRUTAL STRATEGY

Meanwhile, Grievous is eager to carry out Count Dooku's orders and destroy the medical station and the thousands of clones who were injured on the battlefield. Grievous regards such horrific crimes as just another part of war.

## ANAKIN FIGHTS BACK

After a hair-raising passage through the Kaliida Nebula, Shadow Squadron, headed by Anakin, emerges in open space—with *Malevolence* dead ahead on their scopes. The battle is on!

### VEHICLES

**Y-Wing Fighter**

**Kaliida Shoals Medical Station**

### SOUND EFFECTS

The four-legged power droid is called a PLNK-series droid, for the distinctive "plunk" sound it makes.

### NOTABLE CHARACTERS

**Anakin Skywalker**

**Jedi Master Plo Koon**

**General Grievous**

Damaged power feeds overload *Malevolence*'s port-side ion cannon, sending energy cascading back into the dreadnought's internal systems.

## "The care these JEDI show for their troops is a WEAKNESS."

GENERAL GRIEVOUS

# ANAKIN HAS DAMAGED

the enemy ship *Malevolence* and now seeks to destroy it. Before he can reach the ship, however, General Grievous takes Padmé and C-3PO hostage. Frantic to save his wife, Anakin launches a rescue attempt, infiltrating *Malevolence* with Obi-Wan. But Grievous is waiting for them...

## A SINISTER PLOT

With its hyperdrive damaged, the *Malevolence* flees Republic warships. Padmé has been lured to the area, believing that talks are to be held there, and is pulled into the warship.

## DESTROY MALEVOLENCE

### "A PLAN IS ONLY AS GOOD AS THOSE WHO SEE IT THROUGH."

**WORD OF WARNING**

A robo-conductor aboard the *Malevolence*'s rail train warns passengers to "mind the gap."

In the early days of the Clone Wars, many Jedi don partial clone armor as protection on the battlefield and in hopes of forming a closer bond with the troops they now lead in battle.

**VEHICLE**

**Naboo Star Yacht**

**#8**
EPISODE 4, SEASON 1

**AIRDATE**
OCTOBER 17, 2008

**DIRECTOR**
BRIAN KALIN O'CONNELL

**WRITER**
TIM BURNS

### PADMÉ AND ANAKIN REUNITED
Anakin fights his way through the *Malevolence*'s battle droids and finds his wife. After sharing a relieved embrace, the two decide to sabotage the Separatist dreadnaught's navicomputer.

### COLLISION COURSE
Padmé and Anakin's sabotage works. When the *Malevolence*'s crew activates the great ship's hyperdrive, something goes wrong: The ship sets a course that sends it directly into a nearby moon!

Grievous carries the lightsabers of Jedi he has slain. He regards them as trophies as well as weapons with which he hopes to end the careers of more Jedi.

**DROID**

Firefighter Droid

**NOTABLE CHARACTERS**

Padmé Amidala

Obi-Wan Kenobi

**LOCATION**

Dead Moon Of Antar

General Grievous

## "We're DOOMED!"

C-3PO

**UNDER ORDERS** from General Grievous, commando droids attack a Republic listening post on the Rishi Moon. Grievous hopes this will help the Separatists avoid detection ahead of their planned attack on Kamino, the main source of clone production. A group of rookie clone troopers stationed on the moon are the only defense against certain disaster for the Republic war effort.

## DROID ASSAULT

Tougher, faster, and smarter than regular battle droids, commando droids are designed for missions needing both speed and stealth. They arrive on the Rishi Moon with one mission: to seize the Republic's listening post.

A clone trooper's "bucket" is the most important part of his armor, containing a heads-up display, communications gear, sensors, and targeting software.

## ROOKIES

"THE BEST CONFIDENCE BUILDER IS EXPERIENCE."

### NOTABLE CHARACTERS

**Hevy**

**Fives**

**Echo**

**#9**
EPISODE 5, SEASON 1

**AIRDATE**
OCTOBER 24, 2008

**DIRECTOR**
JUSTIN RIDGE

**WRITER**
STEVEN MELCHING

26

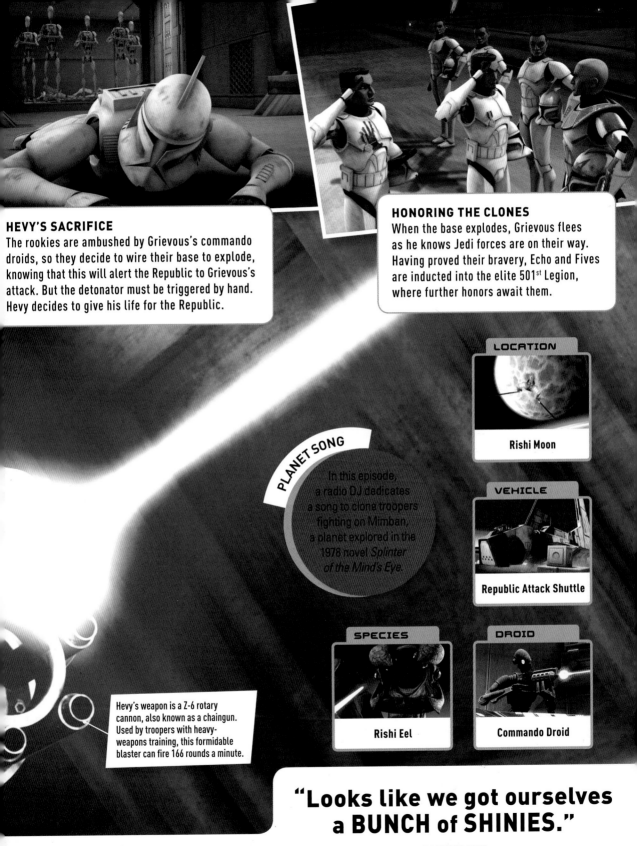

## HEVY'S SACRIFICE

The rookies are ambushed by Grievous's commando droids, so they decide to wire their base to explode, knowing that this will alert the Republic to Grievous's attack. But the detonator must be triggered by hand. Hevy decides to give his life for the Republic.

## HONORING THE CLONES

When the base explodes, Grievous flees as he knows Jedi forces are on their way. Having proved their bravery, Echo and Fives are inducted into the elite 501st Legion, where further honors await them.

**LOCATION**

Rishi Moon

**PLANET SONG**

In this episode, a radio DJ dedicates a song to clone troopers fighting on Mimban, a planet explored in the 1978 novel *Splinter of the Mind's Eye*.

**VEHICLE**

Republic Attack Shuttle

**SPECIES**

Rishi Eel

**DROID**

Commando Droid

Hevy's weapon is a Z-6 rotary cannon, also known as a chaingun. Used by troopers with heavy-weapons training, this formidable blaster can fire 166 rounds a minute.

# "Looks like we got ourselves a BUNCH of SHINIES."

CAPTAIN REX

# DOWNFALL OF A DROID

**ANAKIN AMBUSHES** a Separatist task force at Bothawui, but is nearly killed when his starfighter is wrecked. He awakens to learn R2-D2 is missing: A Trandoshan scavenger, Gha Nachkt, found the astromech and agreed to bring him to Grievous. Anakin must rescue his friend R2 before Grievous digs into the droid's memory and accesses some of the Republic's biggest military secrets.

## R2 IS GONE!
Despite nearly dying when his starfighter is hit by debris, Anakin quickly returns to the battlefield, hunting for any sign of R2-D2. But the droid socket of his wrecked fighter is empty.

"TRUST IN YOUR FRIENDS, AND THEY'LL HAVE REASON TO TRUST IN YOU."

### NOTABLE CHARACTERS

Anakin Skywalker

Ahsoka Tano

Gha Nachkt

Trandoshan Gha Nachkt is native to Dosha, a planet in the same system as the Wookiee world of Kashyyyk.

### TEAM COLORS
R3-S6's black-and-gold color scheme was chosen by supervising director Dave Filoni as a nod to his hometown of Pittsburgh, whose football team, the Steelers wear those colors.

---

**#10**
EPISODE 6, SEASON 1

**AIRDATE**
NOVEMBER 7, 2008

**DIRECTOR**
ROB COLEMAN

**WRITER**
GEORGE KRSTIC

## NO REPLACEMENT
Obi-Wan and Ahsoka do not understand Anakin's attachment to R2, seeing astromechs as interchangeable machines. Yet, to Anakin, there's no replacing R2—particularly not with the error-prone R3-S6.

## ABOARD THE SCAVENGER
Anakin and Ahsoka board Skytop Station in search of R2. The ship's captain, Gha Nachkt, has hidden R2 and promised him to General Grievous. Will Anakin find his droid in time?

### NASTY SMELLS
Certain sounds—and Ahsoka's reactions—make it clear that Gha Nachkt's hygiene leaves a lot to be desired.

**LOCATION**

Bothawui Prime

Anakin covers his Jedi tunic with a poncho to appear like an ordinary galactic citizen seeking a replacement for a lost droid. But there's no hiding the significance of an ignited lightsaber.

**DROID**

TT-8L Gatekeeper Droid

**VEHICLES**

Jedi Starfighter

*Vulture's Claw*

AT-TE

## "You'll be SORRY you ever came aboard my SHIP, Jedi."
GHA NACHKT

**ANAKIN TRACKS** a distress call from captured R2-D2 to a secret Separatist listening post called Skytop Station. He races off in the *Twilight* with Ahsoka to rescue his droid friend. When they reach the station they realize that R3-S6, the droid working with Anakin in R2's absence, is actually a spy for General Grievous and is putting their lives in danger.

## DROID SECRETS

Grievous takes R2-D2 from scavenger Gha Nachkt and digs into the astromech's memory banks on Skytop Station. He is eager to retrieve the Republic's military secrets.

### FREIGHTER SEATS

If the seats on Gha Nachkt's freighter, the *Vulture's Claw*, look familiar, it's because they are similar to those in the cockpit of the *Millennium Falcon*.

Grievous cannot feel the Force, but his cybernetic speed and training as a warrior make him a match for an inexperienced Padawan, such as Ahsoka.

# DUEL OF THE DROIDS

**"YOU HOLD ONTO FRIENDS BY KEEPING YOUR HEART A LITTLE SOFTER THAN YOUR HEAD."**

## NOTABLE CHARACTERS

**General Grievous**

**R2-D2**

**R3-S6**

| LOCATION | DROID | VEHICLE |
|---|---|---|
|  |  |  |
| **Skytop Station** | **MagnaGuard** | **Soulless One** |

**#11**
EPISODE 7, SEASON 1

**AIRDATE**
NOVEMBER 14, 2008

**DIRECTOR**
ROB COLEMAN

**WRITERS**
KEVIN CAMPBELL
HENRY GILRO

**RESCUING R2**
Grievous sends R2 to captivity, escorted by bodyguards. They are met by Anakin, who has come to rescue the droid. He reduces the guards to scrap metal in a dazzling display of Jedi combat skills.

**TRAITOR DROID**
Anakin and the clones rig Skytop Station with explosives. As the Jedi race to escape from the doomed station, R3 obeys his real master, Grievous, and moves to stop them. This leads to a mechanical showdown with R2-D2!

Ahsoka is capable and brave, but the revelation that R3 is a traitor leaves her rattled—and a Jedi must be calm to let the Force flow through her and guide her actions.

**"Sorry to interrupt your playtime, GRUMPY, but wouldn't you prefer a CHALLENGE?"**

AHSOKA TANO

**WITH HIS PEOPLE** starving, a desperate Senator Onaconda Farr betrays his old friend Padmé. Nute Gunray has promised to deliver food to Rodia in exchange for Padmé. But what Farr doesn't know is that Nute intends to execute her. Nute has wanted revenge since his failed blockade of Naboo a decade ago. It falls upon C-3PO and Jar Jar Binks to rescue the senator.

## A CUNNING DISGUISE
When Padmé doesn't return to the ship after visiting Farr on Rodia, Jar Jar dons a Jedi robe and sets out to rescue her. C-3PO knows the well-meaning Gungan is headed for another disaster.

# BOMBAD JEDI

### "HEROES ARE MADE BY THE TIMES."

Trade Federation Viceroy Nute Gunray has despised Padmé Amidala ever since she helped defeat him at Naboo. Now, thanks to the desperation of Rodia's senator, he will have his revenge.

## NOTABLE CHARACTERS

**Nute Gunray**

**Jar Jar Binks**

**Senator Onaconda Farr**

## DROID

**Crab Droid**

| #12 | AIRDATE | DIRECTOR | WRITERS |
|---|---|---|---|
| EPISODE 8, SEASON 1 | NOVEMBER 21, 2008 | JESSE YEH | KEVIN RUBIO, HENRY GILROY, STEVEN MELCH |

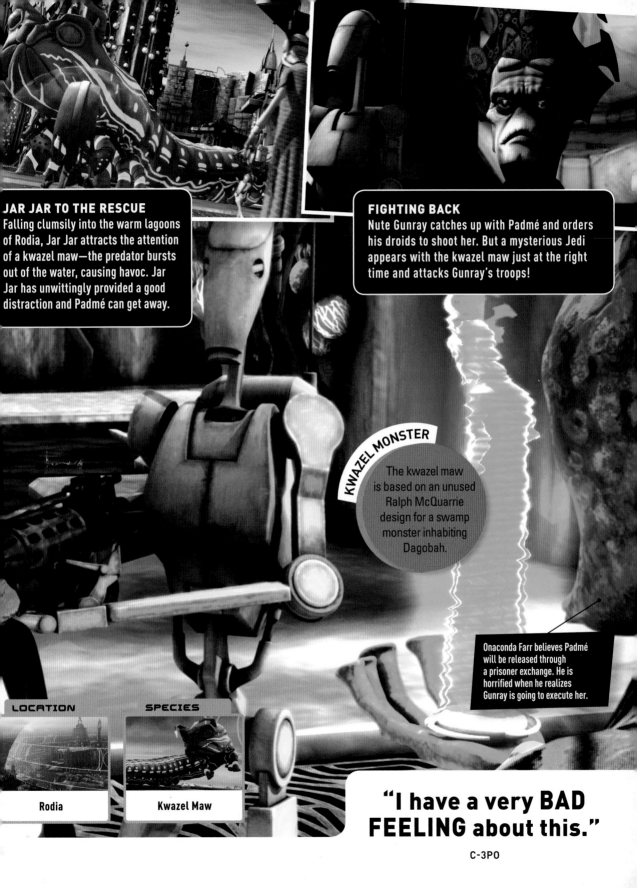

## JAR JAR TO THE RESCUE
Falling clumsily into the warm lagoons of Rodia, Jar Jar attracts the attention of a kwazel maw—the predator bursts out of the water, causing havoc. Jar Jar has unwittingly provided a good distraction and Padmé can get away.

## FIGHTING BACK
Nute Gunray catches up with Padmé and orders his droids to shoot her. But a mysterious Jedi appears with the kwazel maw just at the right time and attacks Gunray's troops!

### KWAZEL MONSTER
The kwazel maw is based on an unused Ralph McQuarrie design for a swamp monster inhabiting Dagobah.

Onaconda Farr believes Padmé will be released through a prisoner exchange. He is horrified when he realizes Gunray is going to execute her.

**LOCATION**

Rodia

**SPECIES**

Kwazel Maw

## "I have a very BAD FEELING about this."

C-3PO

## LLOWING NUTE GUNRAY'S

...pt on Padmé Amidala's life, Ahsoka and
...nara Unduli escort Gunray back to Coruscant
...swer for his crimes. But Count Dooku orders
... Ventress to attack the Jedi cruiser and free
...ay. Ahsoka and Luminara battle Ventress and her
...ds, unaware that there is a traitor aboard who has
... bribed by Dooku to ensure Gunray's escape.

### GUNRAY CAPTURED

After his crimes on Rodia, the Republic transfers
Gunray to Coruscant under tight security. He is
transported on a Jedi cruiser with a Jedi Master,
clone troops, and a senate guard unit aboard.

Captain Argyus's family has served
honorably in the Senate Guard for
generations. Yet Faro Argyus wants
wealth, not honor.

"IGNORE YOUR INSTINCTS AT YOUR PERIL."

### STUDIOUS CLONE

CC-1004 took
the nickname "Gree"
as tribute to his interest
in alien cultures. The
Gree are an ancient
species from the
Outer Rim.

**#13**
EPISODE 9, SEASON 1

**AIRDATE**
DECEMBER 5, 2008

**DIRECTOR**
DAVE FILONI

**WRITER**
PAUL DINI

## ASAJJ VS. LUMINARA
Battle droids led by Ventress attack the cruiser; then Ventress lures Luminara away from the detention level as they duel.

## TRAITOR IN OUR MIDST
Ventress's diversion allows Captain Argyus to act. Dooku has paid him a fortune to spring Gunray from prison so that he cannot reveal Separatist secrets in a Republic court.

**DROID**

**Treadwell Droid**

**NOTABLE CHARACTERS**

**Ahsoka Tano**

**Asajj Ventress**

**Captain Argyus**

**Jedi Master Luminara Unduli**

When Commander Gree expresses shock at Argyus's treason, Argyus mocks him, saying that he wouldn't expect a clone to understand his dislike of a life of servitude.

## "Now you FALL, as all Jedi MUST."

ASAJJ VENTRESS

## JEDI KNIGHT KIT FISTO

tracks the escaped Nute Gunray to the moon
of Vassek, where he meets his former Padawan,
Nahdar Vebb. The two Jedi realize Vassek
is General Grievous's lair—and Nahdar is eager
to take revenge against the Separatist warlord.
Is the young Jedi falling to the dark side?
Are Fisto and Nahdar walking into a trap?

### JEDI IN DARKNESS
Kit congratulates Nahdar for becoming a full-fledged
Jedi Knight, but he soon realizes that war has
caused his old Padawan to give in to anger and fear.

**NOTABLE CHARACTERS**

General Grievous

Kit Fisto

Nahdar Vebb

**SPECIES**

Roggwart

**LOCATION**

Vassek

# LAIR OF GRIEVOUS

"MOST POWERFUL IS HE WHO CONTROLS HIS OWN POWER."

| #14 EPISODE 10, SEASON 1 | AIRDATE DECEMBER 12, 2008 | DIRECTOR ATSUSHI TAKEUCHI | WRITER HENRY GILROY |
|---|---|---|---|

## A DEADLY CONFRONTATION

After following Grievous into his lair and battling a roggwart, Nahdar confronts Grievous alone. The impulsive young Jedi is unaware that he is no match for the cyborg general.

## FIGHTING FREE

With Nahdar destroyed, Kit retreats from Grievous's fortress, calling for help via his astromech R6-H5. Before Kit can escape, he must fight past Grievous's MagnaGuards.

Under Grievous's direction, Gor the Roggwart has been surgically enhanced with exoskeletal armor and cybernetic arms.

### AQUATIC BEINGS

The Jedi ranks include numerous aquatic species. Kit Fisto is a Nautolan from Glee Anselm, while Nahdar Vebb is a Mon Calamari from Mon Cala.

Roggwarts are native to the planet Guiteica, a neighbor of Grievous's homeworld of Kalee. After the invasion of Guiteica, many Kaleesh warlords took baby roggwarts as trophies.

## "In this war, a DANGER there is of LOSING who we are."

YODA

**COUNT DOOKU** escapes a Republic attack but crash-lands on the planet Vanqor, with Anakin and Obi-Wan in hot pursuit. Dooku evades his Jedi pursuers by tricking them into a subterranean nest of aggressive gundarks. However, he is then captured by Hondo Ohnaka and his gang of pirates, who decide to hold the Sith Lord hostage.

### DRAWN INTO A TRAP
On Vanqor, the two Jedi are in the lair of an enormous, angry gundark matriarch. Obi-Wan is amused by Anakin's struggle with the creature, before he dispatches it himself.

# DOOKU CAPTURED

## "THE WINDING PATH TO PEACE IS ALWAYS A WORTHY ONE, REGARDLESS OF HOW MANY TURNS IT TAKES."

Magnetic cuffs keep Dooku bound in a containment field of energy, making it difficult for him to maintain a connection with the Force.

### VICIOUS SPECIES
Gundarks are mentioned (but not seen) in Episode V: *The Empire Strikes Back* and then again in Episode II: *Attack of the Clones.*

### NOTABLE CHARACTERS

**Count Dooku**     **Hondo Ohnaka**

| #15 EPISODE 11, SEASON 1 | AIRDATE JANUARY 2, 2009 | DIRECTOR JESSE YEH | WRITER JULIE SIEGE |
|---|---|---|---|

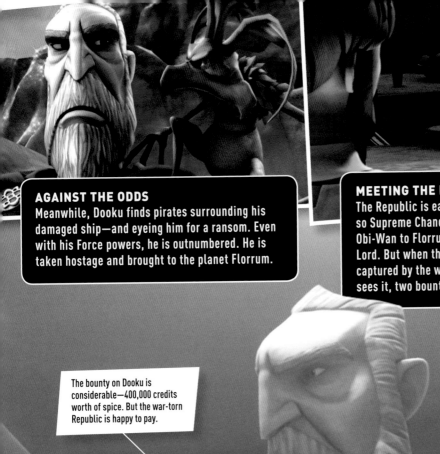

## AGAINST THE ODDS
Meanwhile, Dooku finds pirates surrounding his damaged ship—and eyeing him for a ransom. Even with his Force powers, he is outnumbered. He is taken hostage and brought to the planet Florrum.

## MEETING THE PIRATES
The Republic is eager to capture Count Dooku, so Supreme Chancellor Palpatine sends Anakin and Obi-Wan to Florrum to verify Hondo has the Sith Lord. But when the Jedi arrive, they too are captured by the wily pirate and his gang. As Hondo sees it, two bounties are better than one!

The bounty on Dooku is considerable—400,000 credits worth of spice. But the war-torn Republic is happy to pay.

### PIRATE SHIPS
The ships used by Hondo and his pirates look very much like flying saucers from 1950s space movies.

**VEHICLE**
Flarestar-class Attack Shuttle

**LOCATION**
Vanqor

### SPECIES

Gundarks

Kowakian Monkey-Lizard

## "Obi-Wan Kenobi. I thought I recognized an UNPLEASANT DISTURBANCE in the Force."
COUNT DOOKU

**ANAKIN AND OBI-WAN** wake up in a cell on Florrum with Dooku, having been sedated by Hondo's pirates. They have no choice but to join forces with Dooku to escape. The Republic sends a shuttle loaded with spice to pay Dooku's ransom, but renegade pirates shoot it down, leaving Jar Jar Binks in command of the surviving clone troopers. Is having an addled Gungan in charge of a military operation a wise decision?

### ANAKIN CONFRONTS THE PIRATES
It should be easy for two Jedi and a Sith to escape from a bunch of drunken pirates. But Obi-Wan, Anakin, and Dooku find their attempts repeatedly foiled.

## NOTABLE CHARACTERS

**Stone**

**Hondo Ohnaka**

**Jar Jar Binks**

The clone troopers accompanying Jar Jar to Florrum are members of the elite Coruscant Guard.

# THE GUNGAN GENERAL

## "FAIL WITH HONOR RATHER THAN SUCCEED BY FRAUD."

**#16**
EPISODE 12, SEASON 1

**AIRDATE**
JANUARY 9, 2009

**DIRECTOR**
JUSTIN RIDGE

**WRITER**
JULIE SIEGE

## JAR JAR INTO BATTLE
Riding skalders, Jar Jar, and the clones chase after the pirates who stole the spice for Dooku's ransom. Soon a fierce battle breaks out on the plains of Florrum.

## MAKING AN ESCAPE
When Jar Jar accidentally shuts down the power to Hondo's base, the Jedi and Dooku escape. As Jedi, Anakin and Obi-Wan do not take revenge on the pirates, but will the Sith Lord be so honorable?

### SPECIES

**Skalder**

### LOCATION

**Florrum**

### VEHICLES

**Starhawk Speeder Bike**

**Pirate Speeder Tank**

CC-5869, nicknamed "Stone," often serves with the Diplomatic Escort Group, guarding Republic officials on dangerous missions.

### JAR JAR'S VOICE
Prequel actor Ahmed Best provides the voice for Jar Jar in most episodes, but in this episode, and two others, his vocals are credited to BJ Hughes.

## "MEESA be havin' an idea . . ."
JAR JAR BINKS

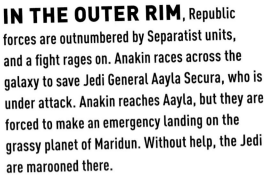

**IN THE OUTER RIM**, Republic forces are outnumbered by Separatist units, and a fight rages on. Anakin races across the galaxy to save Jedi General Aayla Secura, who is under attack. Anakin reaches Aayla, but they are forced to make an emergency landing on the grassy planet of Maridun. Without help, the Jedi are marooned there.

## JEDI IN TROUBLE

With Jedi General Aayla Secura in trouble, Anakin and Ahsoka rush to the rescue. They reach Aayla's cruiser, but come under heavy fire. Anakin is badly injured in a blast and they crash-land on Maridun.

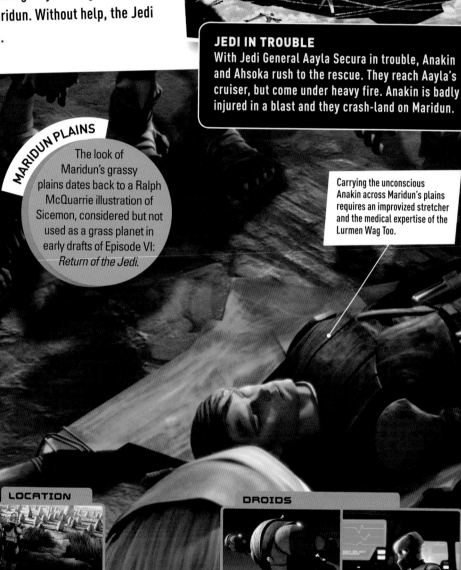

# JEDI CRASH

**"GREED AND FEAR OF LOSS ARE THE ROOTS THAT LEAD TO THE TREE OF EVIL."**

**MARIDUN PLAINS**

The look of Maridun's grassy plains dates back to a Ralph McQuarrie illustration of Sicemon, considered but not used as a grass planet in early drafts of Episode VI: *Return of the Jedi.*

Carrying the unconscious Anakin across Maridun's plains requires an improvised stretcher and the medical expertise of the Lurmen Wag Too.

**LOCATION**

Maridun

**DROIDS**

Rocket Super Battle Droid

2-1B Medical Droid

**#17**
EPISODE 13, SEASON 1

**AIRDATE**
JANUARY 16, 2009

**DIRECTOR**
ROB COLEMAN

**WRITER**
KATIE LUCAS

### STRANDED ON MARIDUN
On Maridun, Captain Rex tends the injured Anakin while Aayla and Ahsoka begin a dangerous night journey across a hostile world in search of help.

### THE NATIVES
Aayla and Ahsoka find a colony of Lurmen—pacifist aliens who have tried to escape the war. Will they come to Anakin's aid?

Maridun's Lurmen arrived from their homeworld of Mygeeto, a Republic target because of its affiliation with the Banking Clan.

**HEAVY BREATHING**
The ventilator Anakin is hooked up to aboard the Jedi cruiser makes the same sound as Darth Vader's breath mask.

**SPECIES**

Mastiff Phalone

**NOTABLE CHARACTERS**

Jedi General Aayla Secura

Lurmen Healer Wag Too

Captain Rex

## "Are all JEDI so RECKLESS?"
ADMIRAL WULLF YULAREN

**THE SEPARATIST** weapons researcher General Lok Durd chooses Maridun as a testing ground for his defoliator tank, which is designed to destroy organic matter while leaving mechanicals unharmed. Anakin, Ahsoka, and Aayla, marooned on the planet, prepare to fight Durd's battle droids, but the Lurmen's pacifist leader refuses to join them, despite the threat to his people's way of life.

### A THREAT TO THE COLONY
Arriving on Maridun, Durd tells the Lurmen that they are now under his "protection." Despite the pacifists' attempts to escape the war, the war has found them.

# DEFENDERS OF PEACE

*"WHEN SURROUNDED BY WAR, ONE MUST EVENTUALLY CHOOSE A SIDE."*

## NOTABLE CHARACTERS

| | | | |
|---|---|---|---|
| **Jedi Master Aayla Secura** | **General Lok Durd** | **Lurmen Leader Tee Watt Kaa** | **Lurmen Healer Wag Too** |

| **#18** EPISODE 14, SEASON 1 | **AIRDATE** JANUARY 23, 2009 | **DIRECTOR** STEWARD LEE | **WRITER** BILL CANTERBURY |
|---|---|---|---|

44

## SWATH OF DESTRUCTION
Durd tests his defoliator on a pair of hapless battle droids, bathing them in fire. They are unharmed—but the surrounding landscape is destroyed. Next, Durd plans to test the defoliator on innocent Lurmen villagers.

## WAR COMES TO THE VILLAGERS
Wag Too watches in horror as droids invade his village. Only when all hope is lost do the Lurmen join the Jedi in defending their home. They are saved, but at what cost to their pacifist beliefs?

Energy tendrils feed the defensive shield set up by the Jedi to protect the Lurmen village.

**DROID**

Recon Droid

**SPECIES**

Carrier Butterfly

**VEHICLES**

Defoliator Tank

Separatist Landing Craft

### LOK DURD
The voice of Lok Durd is supplied by veteran actor George Takei, who played Sulu in *Star Trek*.

## "A strong BELIEF can be more POWERFUL than any ARMY."
AAYLA SECURA

## ANAKIN AND OBI-WAN

arrive on the frozen world of Orto Plutonia to investigate why a Republic base has fallen silent—and discover that the base has been destroyed by ferocious Talz warriors. The shaggy Talz want only to be left alone, but Chairman Chi Cho of neighboring Pantora claims the planet for his own and orders the clones to fight the Talz.

### CHO TAKES CHARGE
Aggressive Chairman Chi Cho claims Orto Plutonia belongs to Pantora, and sees enemies everywhere. Senate protocol gives Cho the right to command Republic troops. The Jedi are helpless to intervene, even though they fear that Cho's commands will lead to tragedy.

### BIG FREEZE
The Freeco bikes that the clones ride in this episode are so named for their ability to function in the freezing cold.

# TRESPASS

## "ARROGANCE DIMINISHES WISDOM."

**LOCATION**

Orto Plutonia

**VEHICLE**

Freeco Bike

The Talz ride snow cats called narglatches in battle, and make use of their bones, meat, and hides in village life.

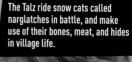

| #19 EPISODE 15, SEASON 1 | AIRDATE JANUARY 30, 2009 | DIRECTOR BRIAN KALIN O'CONNELL | WRITER STEVEN MELCHING |
|---|---|---|---|

## A MYSTERIOUS THREAT
Arriving on Orto Plutonia, the clone troopers find the Republic force there has been destroyed. The Jedi discover that the Talz, who have lived on Orto Plutonia for generations, are responsible.

## MAKING PEACE
After a disastrous attack on the Talz, it falls to Pantoran Senator Riyo Chuchi to seek peace between the Pantorans and the Talz. But is it too late?

**SPECIES**

Narglatch

**NOTABLE CHARACTERS**

Chairman Chi Cho

Senator Riyo Chuchi

Talz Leader Thi-Sen

reeco bikes are formally known as CK-6 swoops, and can ly as fast as 440 kilometers 273 miles) per hour.

**SNOWTROOPERS**
The design of the clone troopers' cold-weather gear dates back to concept art for snowtrooper armor in Episode V: The Empire Strikes Back.

## "I choose to LIVE for my PEOPLE. What do you choose?"
RIYO CHUCHI

**PADMÉ AND JAR JAR** follow the trail of a disease that is killing livestock on Naboo. It leads them to a secret Separatist lab in their homeworld's swamp. This is the lair of Dr. Nuvo Vindi, a mad scientist, who has re-engineered the Blue Shadow Virus. The germ was thought to be extinct; if unleashed, it could eradicate all life in the galaxy.

## BLUE SHADOW VIRUS

### "FEAR IS A DISEASE; HOPE IS ITS ONLY CURE."

### IN THE WATER

Investigating reports of a mysterious virus killing shaaks, Padmé and Jar Jar discover a poison is in the water. This leads them into the swamps—and to Vindi's lab.

### SNACK TIME

The bright blue insects seen in this episode are slug-beetles, prized by Gungans as tasty snacks.

Scientists believed that the pathogen responsible for Candorian Plague—the dreaded Blue Shadow Virus—had been eradicated. Now, Nuvo Vindi has re-engineered it.

#### LOCATION

**Naboo**

#### SPECIES

**Shaak**

**Slug-Beetle**

#### NOTABLE CHARACTERS

**Padmé Amidala**

Jar Jar Binks

**Dr. Nuvo Vindi**

**#20**
EPISODE 17, SEASON 1

**AIRDATE**
FEBRUARY 13, 2009

**DIRECTOR**
GIANCARLO VOLPE

**WRITER**
CRAIG TITLEY

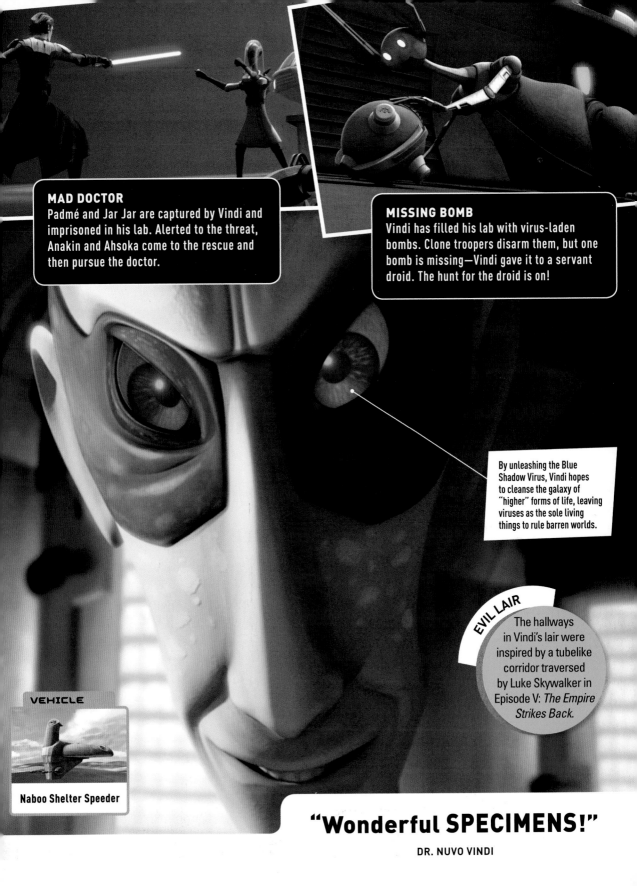

**MAD DOCTOR**
Padmé and Jar Jar are captured by Vindi and imprisoned in his lab. Alerted to the threat, Anakin and Ahsoka come to the rescue and then pursue the doctor.

**MISSING BOMB**
Vindi has filled his lab with virus-laden bombs. Clone troopers disarm them, but one bomb is missing—Vindi gave it to a servant droid. The hunt for the droid is on!

By unleashing the Blue Shadow Virus, Vindi hopes to cleanse the galaxy of "higher" forms of life, leaving viruses as the sole living things to rule barren worlds.

**EVIL LAIR**
The hallways in Vindi's lair were inspired by a tubelike corridor traversed by Luke Skywalker in Episode V: *The Empire Strikes Back*.

**VEHICLE**
Naboo Shelter Speeder

# "Wonderful SPECIMENS!"

DR. NUVO VINDI

**A DROID RELEASES** the Blue Shadow Virus, exposing Padmé, Ahsoka, and several clone troopers within Vindi's lab to the deadly disease. Anakin and Obi-Wan race to the planet Iego in search of the antidote: reeksa root. There they find another trapped population—this one made up of marooned travelers who believe a destructive spirit kills all who try to escape.

### DEADLY EXPOSURE
One of Vindi's droids releases the Blue Shadow Virus inside the lab, endangering Ahsoka, Padmé, and the clones. Unless Anakin and Obi-Wan can find a cure, their friends will die.

Obi-Wan and Anakin's ship, the *Twilight*, must destroy the energy field surrounding Iego before they can return to the lab with the antidote to rescue Padmé and Ahsoka.

The laser web system surrounding Iego consists of a main node on the moon Millius Prime and secondary nodes installed on the smaller moonlets.

**#21**
EPISODE 18, SEASON 1

**AIRDATE**
FEBRUARY 13, 2009

**DIRECTOR**
JESSE YEH

**WRITER**
BRIAN LARSEN

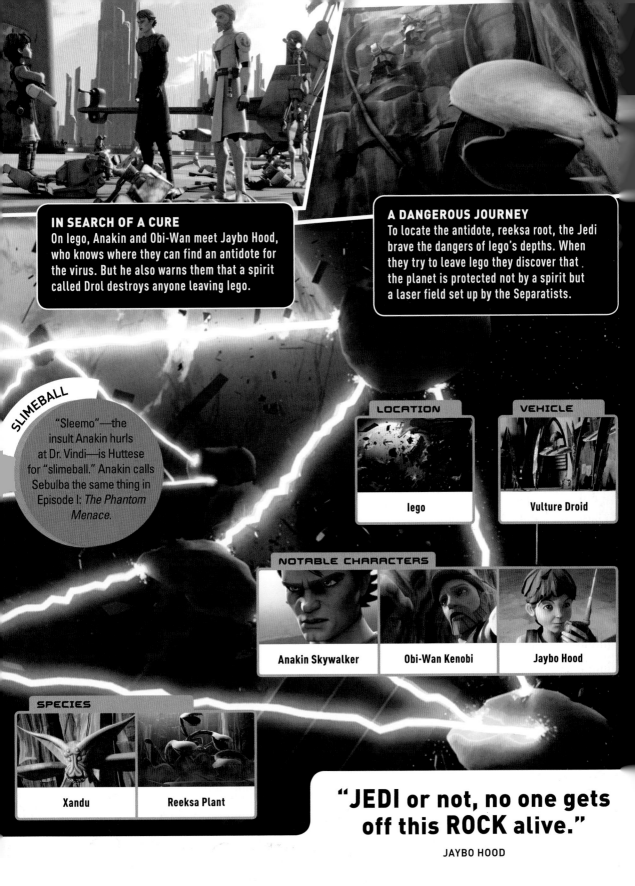

## IN SEARCH OF A CURE

On Iego, Anakin and Obi-Wan meet Jaybo Hood, who knows where they can find an antidote for the virus. But he also warns them that a spirit called Drol destroys anyone leaving Iego.

## A DANGEROUS JOURNEY

To locate the antidote, reeksa root, the Jedi brave the dangers of Iego's depths. When they try to leave Iego they discover that the planet is protected not by a spirit but a laser field set up by the Separatists.

### SLIMEBALL

"Sleemo"—the insult Anakin hurls at Dr. Vindi—is Huttese for "slimeball." Anakin calls Sebulba the same thing in Episode I: *The Phantom Menace*.

### LOCATION

Iego

### VEHICLE

Vulture Droid

### NOTABLE CHARACTERS

Anakin Skywalker

Obi-Wan Kenobi

Jaybo Hood

### SPECIES

Xandu

Reeksa Plant

## "JEDI or not, no one gets off this ROCK alive."

JAYBO HOOD

## AHSOKA'S STARFIGHTERS

try to break the Separatist blockade of the planet Ryloth, but Ahsoka's refusal to follow orders leads to the loss of several of her pilots and leaves Admiral Yularen wounded. Anakin must restore his apprentice's faith in herself and come up with a plan to break the Separatist stranglehold on Ryloth.

### TRICKED BY TUUK
Ahsoka tries to smash through the blockage on Ryloth, but her pilots are caught out when Mar Tuuk surprises them with reinforcements. Tuuk is there to prevent the Republic invading.

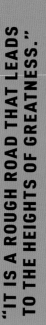

# STORM OVER RYLOTH

"IT IS A ROUGH ROAD THAT LEADS TO THE HEIGHTS OF GREATNESS."

### VEHICLES

**Trade Federation Battleship**

**V-19 Torrent Starfighter**

### NOTABLE CHARACTERS

**Anakin Skywalker**

**Admiral Yularen**

**Mar Tuuk**

**52**

**#22**
EPISODE 19, SEASON 1

**AIRDATE**
FEBRUARY 27, 2009

**DIRECTOR**
BRIAN KALIN
O'CONNELL

**WRITER**
GEORGE KRSTIC

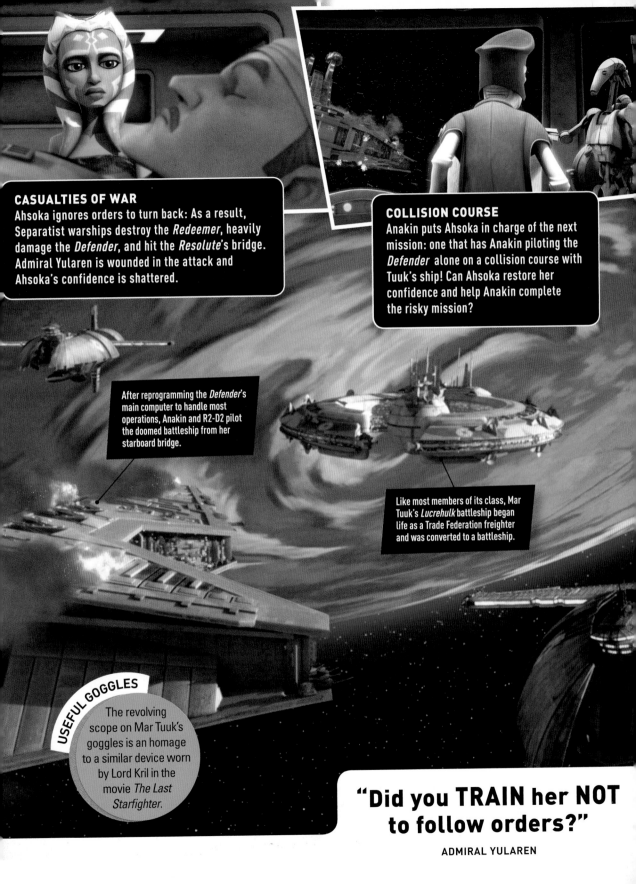

**CASUALTIES OF WAR**
Ahsoka ignores orders to turn back: As a result, Separatist warships destroy the *Redeemer*, heavily damage the *Defender*, and hit the *Resolute*'s bridge. Admiral Yularen is wounded in the attack and Ahsoka's confidence is shattered.

**COLLISION COURSE**
Anakin puts Ahsoka in charge of the next mission: one that has Anakin piloting the *Defender* alone on a collision course with Tuuk's ship! Can Ahsoka restore her confidence and help Anakin complete the risky mission?

After reprogramming the *Defender*'s main computer to handle most operations, Anakin and R2-D2 pilot the doomed battleship from her starboard bridge.

Like most members of its class, Mar Tuuk's *Lucrehulk* battleship began life as a Trade Federation freighter and was converted to a battleship.

**USEFUL GOGGLES**
The revolving scope on Mar Tuuk's goggles is an homage to a similar device worn by Lord Kril in the movie *The Last Starfighter*.

## "Did you TRAIN her NOT to follow orders?"
ADMIRAL YULAREN

**OBI-WAN ATTEMPTS** to destroy Separatist proton cannons on Ryloth that are being protected by a shield of Twi'lek hostages. In a devastated Twi'lek town called Nabat, two clone troopers, Boil and Waxer, befriend a young Twi'lek named Numa. Their kindness is repaid when the little girl shows the Republic's forces a way to free the prisoners.

## SHIELDED BY HOSTAGES

To land on Ryloth and rescue the Twi'lek people being held hostage by the Separatists, the Republic's forces must destroy a cluster of proton cannons being shielded by Twi'leks.

Boil's armor bears the colors of the 212th Attack Battalion, led by Commander Cody and Obi-Wan Kenobi. Boil and Waxer are part of Ghost Company, a smaller unit within the battalion.

**COMIC MESSAGE**

A screen in Separatist headquarters says "COMIC RELIEF" in Aurebesh.

# INNOCENTS OF RYLOTH

## "THE COSTS OF WAR CAN NEVER BE TRULY ACCOUNTED FOR."

### NOTABLE CHARACTERS

**Boil**

**Waxer**

**Numa**

**#23**
EPISODE 20, SEASON 1

**AIRDATE**
MARCH 6, 2009

**DIRECTOR**
JUSTIN RIDGE

**WRITER**
HENRY GILROY

## GUTKURRS ATTACK

As the clone troopers search Nabat, a TX-20 droid releases starving gutkurrs to attack the clone troopers and any Twi'leks who may be in hiding. The Jedi and clones appear to be fighting a losing battle.

## GOING UNDERGROUND

While trying to escape, the clone troopers find a Twi'lek girl named Numa who has survived by hiding in tunnels beneath the town. Obi-Wan realizes his troops can use the tunnels to reach the Separatist cannons and save the Twi'leks.

### REUNITED

Boil and Waxer will also take part in the Republic invasion of Geonosis in the episode "Landing at Point Rain."

Thermal detonators are a standard part of all clone trooper equipment, kept on the utility belt for easy access.

### SPECIES

Gutkurr

### VEHICLE

Proton Cannon

# "Nerra, NERRA."

NUMA

## JEDI MASTER MACE

Windu seeks an alliance with Twi'lek freedom fighter Cham Syndulla, hoping that Twi'lek rebels and Republic troops can together break the Separatists' stranglehold on Ryloth's capital city, Lessu. But to get Syndulla's help, Mace must settle a feud between him and the corrupt Senator Orn Free Taa.

### CRUEL MASTERS
The Separatists plan to starve the people of Ryloth and pillage its treasures. Separatist warlord Emir Wat Tambor is the perfect overseer for such cruelty.

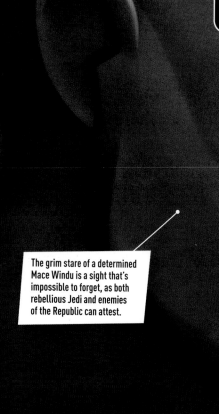

The grim stare of a determined Mace Windu is a sight that's impossible to forget, as both rebellious Jedi and enemies of the Republic can attest.

# LIBERTY ON RYLOTH

"COMPROMISE IS A VIRTUE TO BE CULTIVATED, NOT A WEAKNESS TO BE DESPISED."

## NOTABLE CHARACTERS

**Mace Windu**

**Cham Syndulla**

**Emir Wat Tambor**

## LOCATION

**Ryloth**

| #24 EPISODE 21, SEASON 1 | AIRDATE MARCH 13, 2009 | DIRECTOR ROB COLEMAN | WRITER HENRY GILROY |

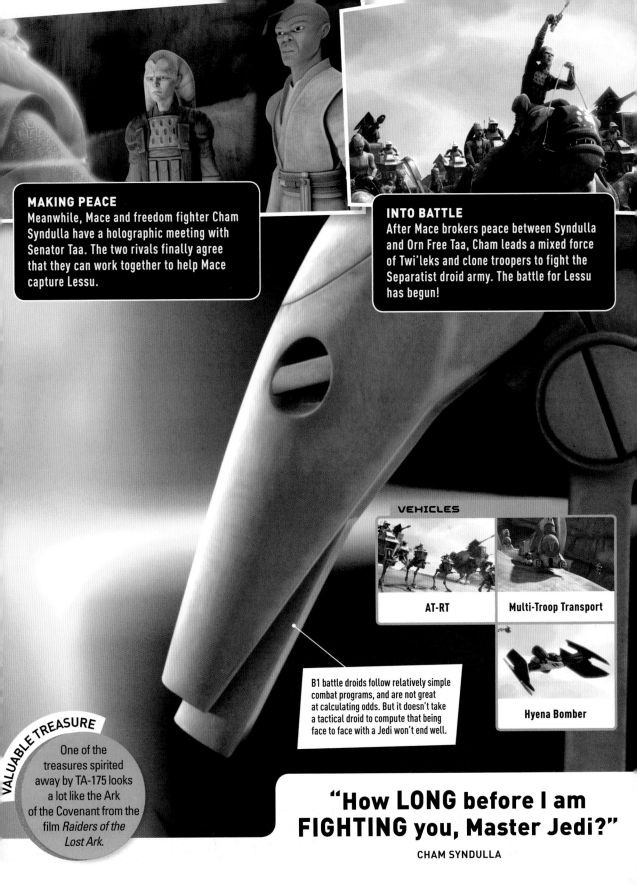

**MAKING PEACE**

Meanwhile, Mace and freedom fighter Cham Syndulla have a holographic meeting with Senator Taa. The two rivals finally agree that they can work together to help Mace capture Lessu.

**INTO BATTLE**

After Mace brokers peace between Syndulla and Orn Free Taa, Cham leads a mixed force of Twi'leks and clone troopers to fight the Separatist droid army. The battle for Lessu has begun!

**VEHICLES**

AT-RT

Multi-Troop Transport

Hyena Bomber

B1 battle droids follow relatively simple combat programs, and are not great at calculating odds. But it doesn't take a tactical droid to compute that being face to face with a Jedi won't end well.

**VALUABLE TREASURE**

One of the treasures spirited away by TA-175 looks a lot like the Ark of the Covenant from the film *Raiders of the Lost Ark*.

## "How LONG before I am FIGHTING you, Master Jedi?"

CHAM SYNDULLA

**AFTER DISOBEYING** orders on the battlefield, Ahsoka is assigned to help strict Jedi Jocasta Nu in the Jedi Archives. But her dull punishment proves eventful: Bounty hunter Cad Bane, his droid Todo 360, and shape-shifter Cato Parasitti break into the Jedi Temple in a plot to steal an ancient Jedi Holocron.

## A DEAL WITH DARTH SIDIOUS

Bane knows breaking into the Jedi Temple is a big deal, so he demands a starfighter and twice his usual pay. His client, the mysterious Darth Sidious, impatiently agrees.

# HOLOCRON HEIST

## "A LESSON LEARNED IS A LESSON EARNED."

### VEHICLE

**Juggernaut**

Bane's breathing tubes feed oxygen directly into his windpipe as a defense against the choking attacks of Force users.

### NOTABLE CHARACTERS

**Cad Bane**

**Cato Parasitti**

**Todo 360**

**Ahsoka Tano**

**Jedi Knight Jocasta Nu**

| #25 EPISODE 1, SEASON 2 | AIRDATE OCTOBER 2, 2009 | DIRECTOR JUSTIN RIDGE | WRITER PAUL DINI |

**BANE'S PLAN**
Bane devises a plot: Parasitti will take the form of a Jedi Master, enter the Archives, and access Temple diagrams. He will then tell Bane and Todo 360 where to break in.

**AHSOKA VS. JOCASTA?**
After Parasitti takes the form of librarian Jocasta Nu, Ahsoka discovers the deception and they duel. But Bane and Todo have already found the right spot to break into the vault.

Access to the Jedi Temple's Holocron vault is normally limited to members of the Jedi Council, as some of the Order's oldest secrets are housed inside.

**A FAMILIAR VOICE**
Todo 360 is voiced by *Buffy the Vampire Slayer* veteran Seth Green, who went on to help create the shows *Robot Chicken* and *Star Wars Detours*.

## "DEEP in the Temple, the INTRUDERS are."

YODA

**AFTER STEALING THE** Holocron, Cad Bane locates Jedi Bolla Ropal, keeper of the Kyber memory crystal. If the Holocron is opened, the Kyber crystal can be used to unlock a secret list of Force-sensitive children in the galaxy—a list that could endanger the future of the Jedi Order. To open the Holocron and complete his mission for Darth Sidious, Bane needs the powers of a Jedi.

## BOLLA ROPAL CAPTURED
Seeking a Jedi to open the Holocron, Bane captures Bolla Ropal and torments him. But Ropal refuses to do the bounty hunter's bidding, even at the cost of his life.

# CARGO OF DOOM

## "OVERCONFIDENCE IS THE MOST DANGEROUS FORM OF CARELESSNESS."

### MEMORY CRYSTALS
The "Kyber crystal" dates back to an early draft script for Episode IV: *A New Hope.* It was resurrected as the Kaiburr crystal in the novel *Splinter of the Mind's Eye.*

### NOTABLE CHARACTERS

**Anakin Skywalker**

**Ahsoka Tano**

**Cad Bane**

**Admiral Yularen**

**Captain Rex**

### VEHICLE

**Bane's Banking Clan Frigate**

**#26**
EPISODE 2, SEASON 2

**AIRDATE**
OCTOBER 2, 2009

**DIRECTOR**
ROB COLEMAN

**WRITER**
GEORGE KRSTIC

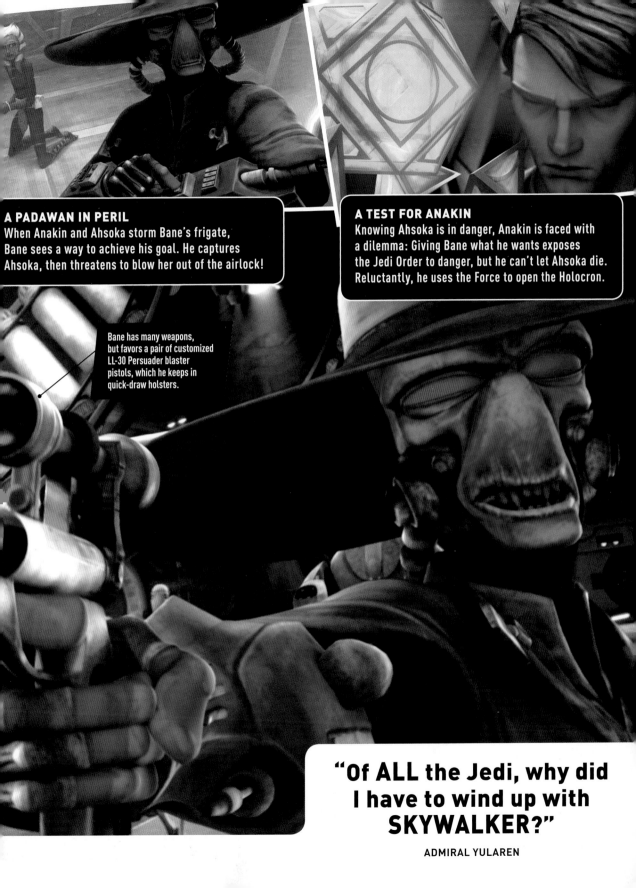

## A PADAWAN IN PERIL
When Anakin and Ahsoka storm Bane's frigate, Bane sees a way to achieve his goal. He captures Ahsoka, then threatens to blow her out of the airlock!

## A TEST FOR ANAKIN
Knowing Ahsoka is in danger, Anakin is faced with a dilemma: Giving Bane what he wants exposes the Jedi Order to danger, but he can't let Ahsoka die. Reluctantly, he uses the Force to open the Holocron.

Bane has many weapons, but favors a pair of customized LL-30 Persuader blaster pistols, which he keeps in quick-draw holsters.

"Of ALL the Jedi, why did I have to wind up with SKYWALKER?"

ADMIRAL YULAREN

# CHILDREN OF THE FORCE

## "THE FIRST STEP TO CORRECTING A MISTAKE IS PATIENCE."

**HAVING STOLEN** the list of Force-sensitive children, Darth Sidious hires Cad Bane to kidnap the infants. Sidious plans to turn the children into spies and servants of the dark side. The Jedi capture Bane on Naboo, but not before some children fall into his clutches. What has the bounty hunter done with these children of the Force?

### KIDNAPPED
On Rodia, Bane hypnotizes the mother of Wee Dunn, a Force-sensitive Rodian child, to persuade her to give up her child. Obi-Wan is right behind the bounty hunter, but Bane escapes with Wee.

Sidious rarely appears to his servants in the flesh, preferring to materialize as a mysterious, but still threatening, hologram.

| #27 EPISODE 3, SEASON 2 | AIRDATE OCTOBER 9, 2009 | DIRECTOR BRIAN KALIN O'CONNELL | WRITERS HENRY GILROY AND WENDY MERICLE |
|---|---|---|---|

## AHSOKA CAPTURES BANE

Bane's luck runs out on Naboo, where Ahsoka captures him. The Jedi interrogate Bane and he reveals the location of the stolen Holocron—but not where the children are.

## ANAKIN TO THE RESCUE

Anakin and Ahsoka discover that Bane has been to Mustafar. They rush to the volcanic world where, under Darth Sidious's command, the children are being prepared for experiments to expose them to the dark side.

### MOBILE CREATURES

The mobile over the Gungan baby's bed in this episode features a sando aqua monster and a colo claw fish—two beasts from Episode I: *The Phantom Menace*.

### NOTABLE CHARACTERS

| Cad Bane | Mace Windu | Darth Sidious |
|---|---|---|

### LOCATIONS

| Mustafar | Black Stall Station | Naboo |
|---|---|---|

### DROID

| Nanny Droid |
|---|

### VEHICLES

| T-6 Shuttle | *Xanadu Blood* |
|---|---|

## "Among the children of the Jedi, there are NO innocents."

DARTH SIDIOUS

# STRANDED ON THE

planet Felucia, three Jedi—Anakin, Ahsoka, and Obi-Wan—join forces with a band of four mercenaries to defend a farming village against the greedy Hondo Ohnaka. Hondo and his pirates want to steal the planet's crop of valuable nysillin spice and they won't let anyone get in their way.

## BOUNTY HUNTERS

"COURAGE MAKES HEROES, BUT TRUST BUILDS FRIENDSHIP."

## DOUBLE DEALING

Obi-Wan thinks mercenary Sugi and her hunters want only to exploit the villagers. His opinion changes when Hondo offers Sugi double her pay to stand aside and she refuses.

### SEVEN SOLDIERS

This episode is an homage to the classic movie *Seven Samurai*. It opens with a title card honoring Akira Kurosawa, the movie's legendary director.

A Frenk mercenary from the planet Gorobei, Rumi Paramita is an expert sniper, favoring an IQA-11 rifle.

| #28 EPISODE 17, SEASON 2 | AIRDATE APRIL 2, 2010 | DIRECTOR STEWARD LEE | WRITER CARL ELLSWORTH |

## EMBO IN ACTION

With the help of the Jedi and mercenaries, the villagers fight back against Hondo's pirates. No fighter is more impressive that Embo, who fights with speed and skill—his hat even doubles as a weapon!

## DANGEROUS DUEL

The pirates' biggest advantage is Hondo's tank, which can fire on the village from a distance. Anakin races to disable it, winding up in a desperate duel with Hondo.

### NOTABLE CHARACTERS

**Embo**

**Sugi**

**Seripas**

**Rumi**

### SPECIES

**Tee-Muss**

### LOCATIONS

**Felucia**

**Vulture Droid Fighter Stall**

Cassis, the village elder, sees the Jedi's arrival as a blessing—now there are seven warriors to protect his people against Hondo's pirates.

## "Speak SOFTLY, and drive a BIG tank."

HONDO OHNAKA

# THE ZILLO BEAST

*"CHOOSE WHAT IS RIGHT, NOT WHAT IS EASY."*

**REPUBLIC FORCES** fighting on Malastare detonate a massive electro-proton bomb designed to devastate the Separatists' mechanical armies. The bomb works—but also frees a giant Zillo beast from underground. The Dugs living on Malastare want Republic forces to help kill the beast, but Mace opposes the decision as killing an innocent creature is not the Jedi way.

**DOCTOR BOLL'S BOMB**
The electro-proton bomb created by scientist Dr. Sionver Boll destroys the Separatists' droid armies. It also creates a huge crater and awakens a Zillo beast, previously known only from Dug legends.

**MOVIE MONSTERS**
Two clone pilots in this episode are named Goji and Rod, and have designs on their helmets evoking Japanese monster movie stars Godzilla and Rodan.

## NOTABLE CHARACTERS

**Doge Nakha Urus**

**Mace Windu**

**R2-D2**

**Dr. Sionver Boll**

## SPECIES

**The Zillo Beast**

**Insectomorphs**

## VEHICLE

**ARC-170 Starfighter**

## LOCATION

**Malastare**

**#29**
EPISODE 18, SEASON 2

**AIRDATE**
APRIL 9, 2010

**DIRECTOR**
GIANCARLO VOLPE

**WRITER**
CRAIG TITLEY

## ON THE LOOSE
The giant creature rampages through Malastare. The Dugs try to poison it with toxic fuel. When this doesn't work, Republic forces try firing stun cannons at the beast to get it under control.

## CAPTURED CREATURE
With the beast finally secure, Anakin and Mace assume the Republic will transport it to a far-off world. Palpatine has other ideas: He wants the giant creature to be studied on Coruscant.

The Zillo beast's scales seem impenetrable to blaster fire and lightsabers. Sionver Boll wonders if studying the beast could help the Republic design tougher armor.

Malastare's fuel is toxic to Zillo beasts: the Dugs' leader says it has been used to kill them in the past.

## THE WILHELM WAIL
When the Zillo beast steps on a clone trooper you hear a "Wilhelm scream." This is an effect begun by sound designer Ben Burtt, and can be heard in all six *Star Wars* movies.

## "It is not the JEDI way to take an INNOCENT life."
MACE WINDU

## ON PALPATINE'S ORDERS,

the captive Zillo beast is brought to Coruscant, where scientist Dr. Sionver Boll hopes its scales can be researched to create better military hardware. After Palpatine orders Boll to kill the beast, it breaks free and rampages across Coruscant, making a beeline for the Senate building and the man who gave his death sentence.

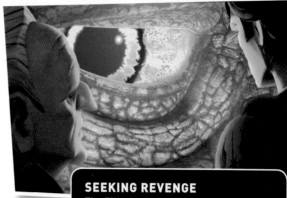

### SEEKING REVENGE
The Zillo beast escapes captivity and rampages across the cityscape of Coruscant. It may be seeking revenge on the man who ordered its torment.

## THE ZILLO BEAST STRIKES BACK
### "THE MOST DANGEROUS BEAST IS THE BEAST WITHIN."

**RETURN OF THE DROIDS**

The hulking labor droids that help Doctor Boll with the Zillo beast are also seen in Episode III: *Revenge of the Sith.*

The Zillo beast's horns are actually ornamental and are chiefly used in courtship displays.

**LOCATION**

Coruscant

**NOTABLE CHARACTERS**

Jedi Master
Aayla Secura

Padmé Amidala

Chancellor Palpatine

| #30 EPISODE 19, SEASON 2 | AIRDATE APRIL 16, 2010 | DIRECTOR STEWARD LEE | WRITER STEVEN MELCHING |
|---|---|---|---|

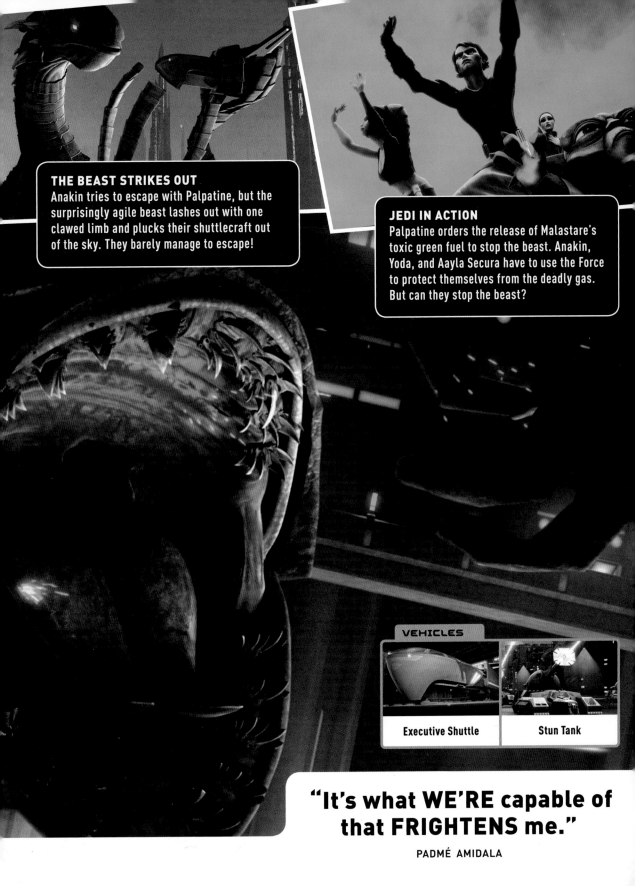

**THE BEAST STRIKES OUT**
Anakin tries to escape with Palpatine, but the surprisingly agile beast lashes out with one clawed limb and plucks their shuttlecraft out of the sky. They barely manage to escape!

**JEDI IN ACTION**
Palpatine orders the release of Malastare's toxic green fuel to stop the beast. Anakin, Yoda, and Aayla Secura have to use the Force to protect themselves from the deadly gas. But can they stop the beast?

**VEHICLES**

Executive Shuttle     Stun Tank

**"It's what WE'RE capable of that FRIGHTENS me."**

PADMÉ AMIDALA

**THE JEDI HAVE** recruited Padmé to spy on her old flame, Senator Rush Clovis, who they suspect is working with the Separatists. When Padmé travels with Clovis and a disguised Anakin on a secret mission to Cato Neimoidia, she becomes caught up in Clovis's illegal plots with Senator Lott Dod.

## A SECRET MEETING

A summons from the Jedi Council ruins Anakin and Padmé's evening. The Council wants her to spy on her old boyfriend, Senator Clovis. She agrees to go with Clovis when he asks her to accompany him on a trip to visit Senator Lott Dod on Cato Neimoidia. A jealous Anakin goes along in disguise.

Lott Dod is the Trade Federation's senator. His Separatist loyalties are not a secret, but he is allowed to serve on Coruscant because his business is vital to galactic trade.

**GRAND ART**

In Lott Dod's palace you can spot a painting of a Neimoidian riding a kaadu that looks a lot like Jacques-Louis David's classic portrait *Napoleon Crossing the Alps.*

# SENATE SPY

## "A TRUE HEART SHOULD NEVER BE DOUBTED."

**NOTABLE CHARACTERS**

Padmé Amidala

Senator Rush Clovis

Senator Lott Dod

**#31**
EPISODE 4, SEASON 2

**AIRDATE**
OCTOBER 16, 2009

**DIRECTOR**
STEWARD LEE

**WRITER**
MELINDA HSU

70

## CAUGHT IN THE ACT

On Cato Neimoidia, Padmé discovers Dod is negotiating with Clovis to fund a droid factory. She downloads the plans, but soon falls ill—Dod has poisoned her and hopes to use the antidote to blackmail Clovis into giving him a better deal.

## PADMÉ IN PERIL

Clovis is angry when he discovers Padmé's treachery, but is determined to save her. He threatens Dod with a blaster, demanding the antidote. Who will save Padmé?

Rush Clovis is a high-ranking member of the Banking Clan, which has financed much of the Separatist military build-up, at a huge profit.

**LOCATION**

Cato Neimoidia

**VEHICLE**

Naboo Star Skiff

## "Duty comes FIRST— ESPECIALLY in wartime."

PADMÉ AMIDALA

# ANAKIN, OBI-WAN,

and Ki-Adi-Mundi lead a massive Republic invasion of the planet Geonosis, whose factories are once again turning out weapons and droids for the Separatists. In the fierce fighting, both Anakin and Obi-Wan are shot down, and must fight for their lives against Geonosian forces.

## GUNSHIPS ON GEONOSIS
The Republic launches an assault on Geonosis, intending to shut down its factories for good. As Y-wings strafe ground targets, gunships race for the surface, dodging bursts of artillery fire.

# LANDING AT POINT RAIN

## "BELIEVE IN YOURSELF OR NO ONE ELSE WILL."

### LOCATION

**Geonosis**

### NOTABLE CHARACTERS

**Anakin Skywalker**

**Obi-Wan Kenobi**

**Jedi Master Ki-Adi-Mundi**

### VEHICLES

**Republic Dropship**

**Geonosian Starfighter**

**#32**
EPISODE 5, SEASON 2

**AIRDATE**
NOVEMBER 4, 2009

**DIRECTOR**
BRIAN KALIN O'CONNELL

**WRITER**
BRIAN LARSEN

**GEONOSIS MUST FALL!**
The fighting rages on the ground, with clone troopers advancing and battling Geonosian drones at close quarters. Despite mounting casualties, the Jedi and clones push on.

**WORKING TOGETHER**
Anakin and Ahsoka lead the mission to destroy the shield generator protecting the droid factories. The Jedi face a difficult task—every step they take is contested by battle droids.

Flame troopers have insulated body gloves, which resist heat and are chilled by coolant reservoirs.

**A D-DAY SALUTE**
The shot of Anakin and his troops charging the Geonosian troops in this episode is an homage to the 1962 D-Day classic movie *The Longest Day*.

Flame troopers lay down sheets of flame with their BT X-42 heavy flamethrowers.

**"There is no such thing as LUCK."**
KI-ADI-MUNDI

## AHSOKA JOINS Luminara
Unduli's Padawan, Barriss Offee, in a risky plan to infiltrate a Separatist droid foundry. When the two Padawans get lost and fail their mission, they accept that they must sacrifice their lives to destroy the foundry—a decision Luminara accepts but Anakin cannot. Will Anakin be able to rescue them from their fate?

### A DOUBLE ATTACK
While Ahsoka and Barriss sneak into the catacombs beneath the foundry to plant bombs, Anakin and Luminara plan a frontal attack to divert the Separatists' attention.

**WEAPONS FACTORY**

"NO GIFT IS MORE PRECIOUS THAN TRUST."

Barriss is prepared to die in the rubble. She has done her duty, as Luminara taught her, and will sacrifice herself if necessary to save countless lives.

**VEHICLE**
Super Tank

**DROID**
Droideka

**NOTABLE CHARACTERS**
Ahsoka Tano

Barriss Offee

Jedi Master Luminara Unduli

Anakin Skywalker

**#33**
EPISODE 6, SEASON 2

**AIRDATE**
NOVEMBER 13, 2009

**DIRECTOR**
GIANCARLO VOLPE

**WRITER**
BRIAN LARSEN

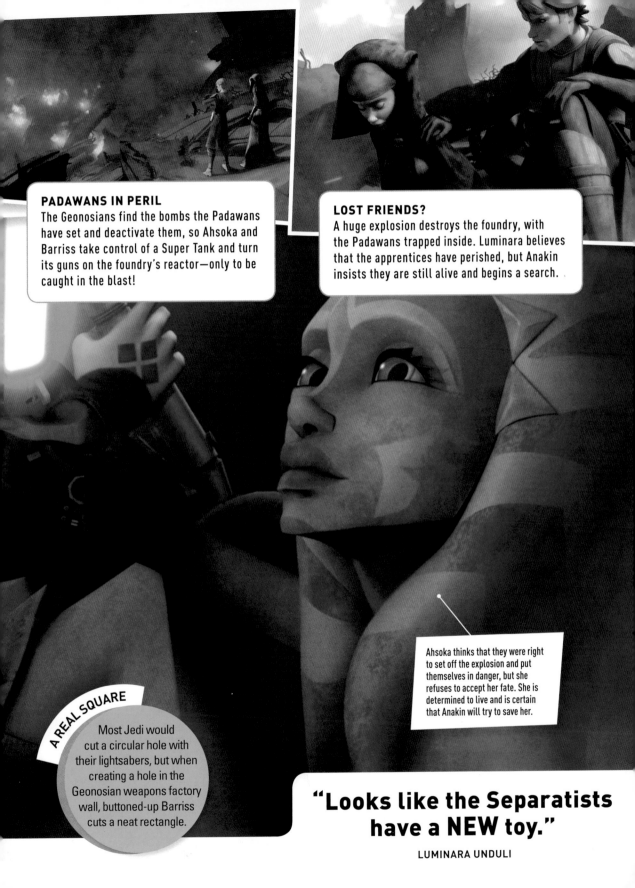

## PADAWANS IN PERIL
The Geonosians find the bombs the Padawans have set and deactivate them, so Ahsoka and Barriss take control of a Super Tank and turn its guns on the foundry's reactor—only to be caught in the blast!

## LOST FRIENDS?
A huge explosion destroys the foundry, with the Padawans trapped inside. Luminara believes that the apprentices have perished, but Anakin insists they are still alive and begins a search.

Ahsoka thinks that they were right to set off the explosion and put themselves in danger, but she refuses to accept her fate. She is determined to live and is certain that Anakin will try to save her.

## A REAL SQUARE
Most Jedi would cut a circular hole with their lightsabers, but when creating a hole in the Geonosian weapons factory wall, buttoned-up Barriss cuts a neat rectangle.

## "Looks like the Separatists have a NEW toy."
LUMINARA UNDULI

**LUMINARA** disappears after tracking the Separatist leader and Archduke of Geonosis, Poggle the Lesser, to a subterranean temple. Following her lead, Anakin and Obi-Wan discover Poggle is hiding in the lair of Karina the Great, the secret Geonosian Queen, who uses parasitic brain worms to re-animate Geonosian corpses. How can Anakin and Obi-Wan rescue Luminara from enemies that are already dead?

## DARK LABYRINTH

As they track Luminara, Anakin and Obi-Wan must lead their troopers through a pitch-black labyrinth where none of them can tell what might be waiting for them around the next corner.

## MILE MEASURES

In this episode, Obi-Wan says "miles" —a rare exception to the usual rule of using metric measurements in *Star Wars*.

Karina believes herself secure in the depths of her royal nest, where she is served by lesser Geonosian nobles such as Poggle and a retinue of servants and warriors.

The Archduke of Geonosis, Poggle is a leading Separatist with extensive dealings with the rest of the galaxy. But few know he takes his orders from an unseen ruler.

# LEGACY OF TERROR

## "SOMETIMES, ACCEPTING HELP IS HARDER THAN OFFERING IT."

| #34 EPISODE 7, SEASON 2 | AIRDATE NOVEMBER 20, 2009 | DIRECTOR STEWARD LEE | WRITER EOGHAN MAHONY |

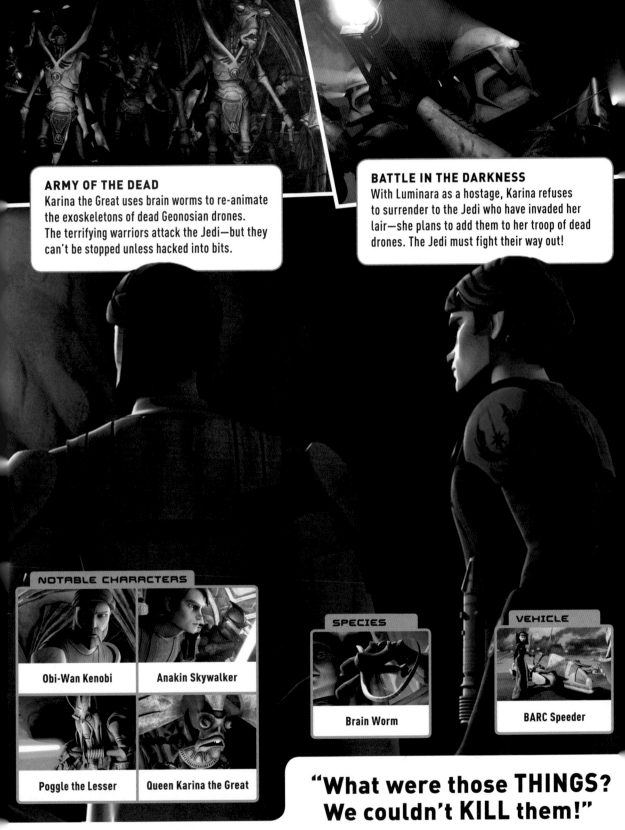

## ARMY OF THE DEAD

Karina the Great uses brain worms to re-animate the exoskeletons of dead Geonosian drones. The terrifying warriors attack the Jedi—but they can't be stopped unless hacked into bits.

## BATTLE IN THE DARKNESS

With Luminara as a hostage, Karina refuses to surrender to the Jedi who have invaded her lair—she plans to add them to her troop of dead drones. The Jedi must fight their way out!

### NOTABLE CHARACTERS

Obi-Wan Kenobi

Anakin Skywalker

Poggle the Lesser

Queen Karina the Great

### SPECIES

Brain Worm

### VEHICLE

BARC Speeder

## "What were those THINGS? We couldn't KILL them!"

ANAKIN SKYWALKER

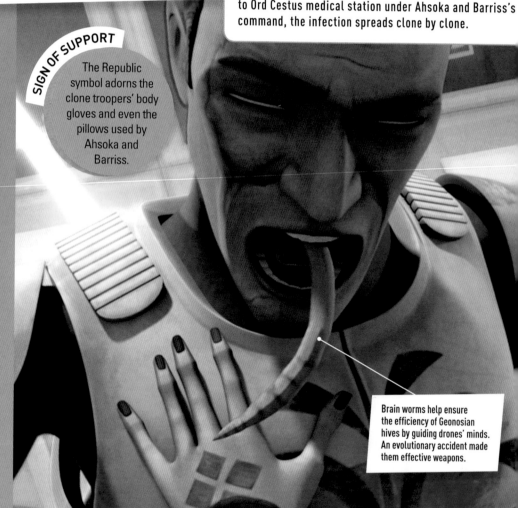

## AHSOKA AND BARRISS

Offee accompany the clone troopers of Tango Company on a mission to Ord Cestus medical station. However, brain worms have made their way onto their ship, and they begin to infect the troopers. While Anakin frantically tries to find a way to neutralize the worms, Ahsoka must separate friend from foe.

### WORMED A WAY IN

Clone trooper Scythe is infected by a brain worm on Geonosis. Obeying its orders, he brings more brain worm eggs aboard the ship. While the vessel makes its way to Ord Cestus medical station under Ahsoka and Barriss's command, the infection spreads clone by clone.

# BRAIN INVADERS

## "ATTACHMENT IS NOT COMPASSION."

**SIGN OF SUPPORT**

The Republic symbol adorns the clone troopers' body gloves and even the pillows used by Ahsoka and Barriss.

Brain worms help ensure the efficiency of Geonosian hives by guiding drones' minds. An evolutionary accident made them effective weapons.

**#35**
EPISODE 8, SEASON 2

**AIRDATE**
DECEMBER 4, 2009

**DIRECTOR**
STEWARD LEE

**WRITER**
ANDREW KREISBERG

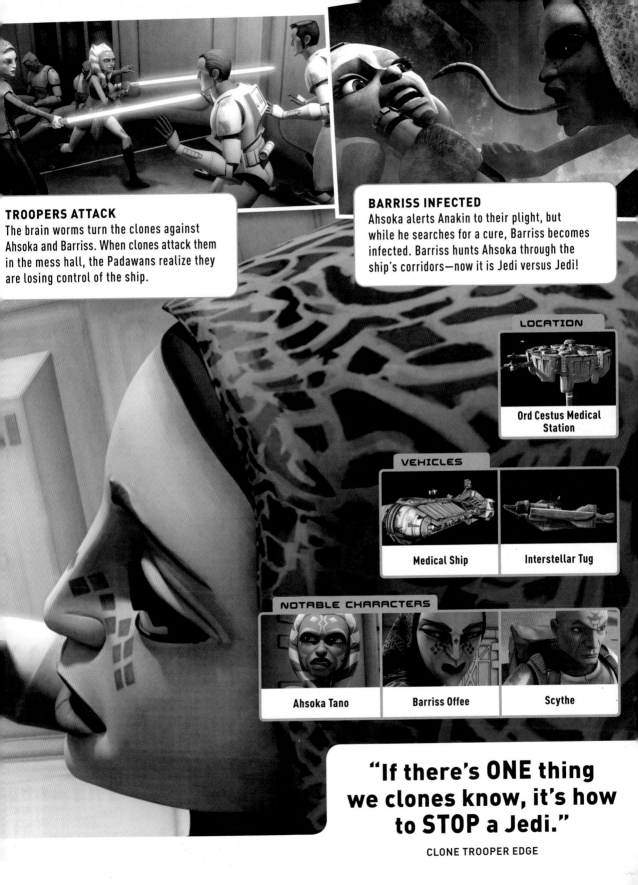

## TROOPERS ATTACK
The brain worms turn the clones against Ahsoka and Barriss. When clones attack them in the mess hall, the Padawans realize they are losing control of the ship.

## BARRISS INFECTED
Ahsoka alerts Anakin to their plight, but while he searches for a cure, Barriss becomes infected. Barriss hunts Ahsoka through the ship's corridors—now it is Jedi versus Jedi!

**LOCATION**

Ord Cestus Medical Station

**VEHICLES**

Medical Ship

Interstellar Tug

**NOTABLE CHARACTERS**

Ahsoka Tano

Barriss Offee

Scythe

## "If there's ONE thing we clones know, it's how to STOP a Jedi."
CLONE TROOPER EDGE

**GENERAL GRIEVOUS** has captured Jedi Master Eeth Koth! Anakin, Obi-Wan, and Adi Gallia race off to rescue their colleague. Obi-Wan allows his ship to be captured by Grievous while Anakin and Adi try to slip through the cyborg general's defenses. The Jedi are walking into Grievous's trap—so Obi-Wan is in great danger!

### KOTH CAPTURED

Eeth Koth and his Jedi cruiser, the *Steadfast*, are patroling the Outer Rim when Grievous attacks. Koth is overpowered by the general, who broadcasts his capture to the Jedi. Koth manages to reveal his location to the Jedi through sign language on the holotransmission.

# GRIEVOUS INTRIGUE

## "FOR EVERYTHING YOU GAIN, YOU LOSE SOMETHING ELSE."

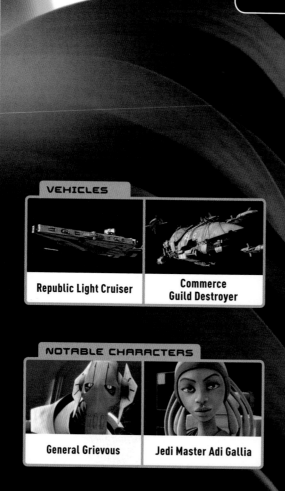

### VEHICLES

Republic Light Cruiser

Commerce Guild Destroyer

### NOTABLE CHARACTERS

General Grievous

Jedi Master Adi Gallia

**#36**
EPISODE 9, SEASON 2

**AIRDATE**
JANUARY 1, 2010

**DIRECTOR**
GIANCARLO VOLPE

**WRITER**
BEN EDLUND

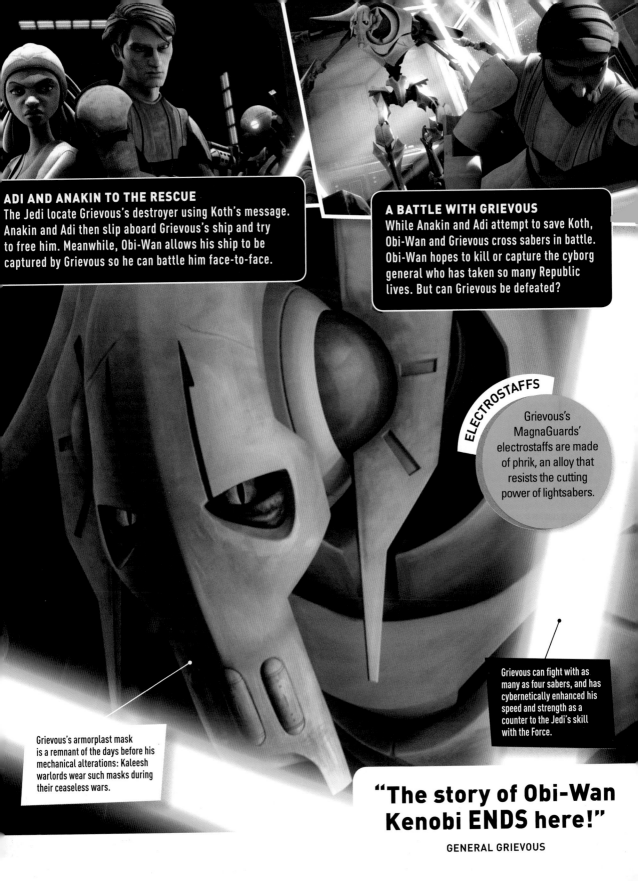

**ADI AND ANAKIN TO THE RESCUE**
The Jedi locate Grievous's destroyer using Koth's message. Anakin and Adi then slip aboard Grievous's ship and try to free him. Meanwhile, Obi-Wan allows his ship to be captured by Grievous so he can battle him face-to-face.

**A BATTLE WITH GRIEVOUS**
While Anakin and Adi attempt to save Koth, Obi-Wan and Grievous cross sabers in battle. Obi-Wan hopes to kill or capture the cyborg general who has taken so many Republic lives. But can Grievous be defeated?

**ELECTROSTAFFS**

Grievous's MagnaGuards' electrostaffs are made of phrik, an alloy that resists the cutting power of lightsabers.

Grievous can fight with as many as four sabers, and has cybernetically enhanced his speed and strength as a counter to the Jedi's skill with the Force.

Grievous's armorplast mask is a remnant of the days before his mechanical alterations: Kaleesh warlords wear such masks during their ceaseless wars.

# "The story of Obi-Wan Kenobi ENDS here!"

GENERAL GRIEVOUS

## OBI-WAN AND CAPTAIN

Rex's troopers land on the planet Saleucami in pursuit of General Grievous. Injured in battle, Rex is left on a farm to recover. Rex discovers that the farmer, Cut Lawquane, is in fact a deserter from the clone army. He now lives a very different life from a clone trooper, with a family of his own.

### A CLONE DOWN

After a commando droid shoots Rex, soldiers in his squad leave him at the Lawquane farmhouse to recover while they continue their hunt for Grievous.

The Lawquane farmhouse is a ramshackle creation of wood, scraps, and starship parts.

# THE DESERTER

**"IT IS THE QUEST FOR HONOR THAT MAKES ONE HONORABLE."**

### NOTABLE CHARACTERS

**Captain Rex**

**Cut Lawquane**

**Suu Lawquane**

### SPECIES

**Eopie**

### LOCATION

**Saleucami**

**#37**
EPISODE 10, SEASON 2

**AIRDATE**
JANUARY 1, 2010

**DIRECTOR**
ROBERT DALVA

**WRITER**
CARL ELLSWORTH

**LIFE CHOICES**
While at the farm with Cut Lawquane and his family, Rex recognizes Cut as a deserter and accuses him of abandoning his duty. But Cut says he has chosen a life that is about more than killing.

**DROIDS ATTACK**
Later, when the farmhouse is attacked by commando droids, Cut and Rex work together to defeat them. The next day, Rex has to rejoin his soldiers, but will he turn in Cut as a deserter?

**FUN AND GAMES**
Cut and Rex play dejarik, a holographic game akin to chess. It is also played by Chewbacca and R2-D2 in Episode IV: *A New Hope*.

Suu Lawquane was raising two children alone before she met Cut—a man with a mysterious past, yearning for a family to call his own.

## "I have a DUTY, you're right. But it's to my FAMILY."

CUT LAWQUANE

**AFTER LOSING** her lightsaber to a pickpocket in the slums of Coruscant, Ahsoka teams up with Tera Sinube, an elderly Jedi who is an expert on the Coruscant underworld. Searching for Ahsoka's lost saber, the two Jedi are drawn into a dramatic chase that teaches Ahsoka a valuable lesson about patience.

## SLOW GOING

Ahsoka is anxious to find her lightsaber and finds Sinube's methods too slow. But the wise Sinube teaches Ahsoka that speed is not as important as knowing where to go.

**PHOTO RECALL**

One of the mugshots Ahsoka studies when searching for Cassie is that of Brea Tonnika, seen with her sister, Senni, in the cantina in Episode IV: *A New Hope.*

Police droids patrol many areas of Coruscant and other advanced worlds. While they have combat programming, their primary function is to prevent injuries to bystanders at potential crime scenes.

# LIGHTSABER LOST

"EASY ISN'T ALWAYS SIMPLE."

**VEHICLE**

Hovertrain

**DROID**

Police Droid

**NOTABLE CHARACTERS**

Ahsoka Tano

Jedi Master Tera Sinube

Cassie Cryar

**#38**
EPISODE 11, SEASON 2

**AIRDATE**
JANUARY 22, 2010

**DIRECTOR**
GIANCARLO VOLPE

**WRITER**
DREW Z. GREENBER

**A HIGH-LEVEL CHASE**
The two Jedi discover Ahsoka's saber is in the hands of Cassie Cryar and her partner-in-crime, Ione Marcy. Cryar leads Ahsoka on a chase through the dizzying heights of Coruscant.

**SINUBE'S SKILL**
Cornered by the Jedi, Cassie takes hostages aboard a hovertrain, but Sinube appears and shows off his combat skills. Ahsoka gets her weapon back, but has she learnt Sinube's lesson?

Cassie Cryar's natural Terellian agility allows her to wield a lightsaber with a relative degree of skill —for a non-Jedi, that is.

**SINUBE DESIGN**
The design of the Cosian Jedi Tera Sinube was originally proposed for a senator in Episode I: *The Phantom Menace*.

**"For a guy who moves SLOW, you always seem to get AHEAD of me."**
AHSOKA TANO

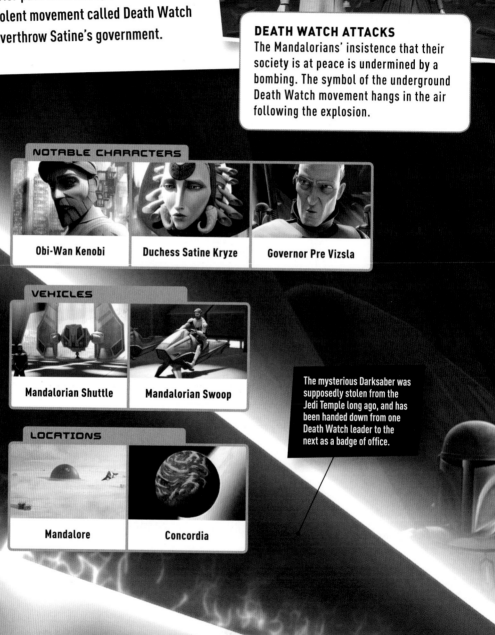

**OBI-WAN VISITS** Mandalore, to investigate recent attacks by warriors in Mandalorian armor on Republic targets. The planet's ruler is Duchess Satine—who is also Obi-Wan's lost love. Satine claims her planet's warrior past is no more, but the two discover a violent movement called Death Watch is trying to overthrow Satine's government.

## DEATH WATCH ATTACKS
The Mandalorians' insistence that their society is at peace is undermined by a bombing. The symbol of the underground Death Watch movement hangs in the air following the explosion.

# THE MANDALORE PLOT

## "IF YOU IGNORE THE PAST, YOU JEOPARDIZE THE FUTURE."

### NOTABLE CHARACTERS

**Obi-Wan Kenobi**

**Duchess Satine Kryze**

**Governor Pre Vizsla**

### VEHICLES

**Mandalorian Shuttle**

**Mandalorian Swoop**

The mysterious Darksaber was supposedly stolen from the Jedi Temple long ago, and has been handed down from one Death Watch leader to the next as a badge of office.

### LOCATIONS

**Mandalore**

**Concordia**

**#39**
EPISODE 12, SEASON 2

**AIRDATE**
JANUARY 29, 2010

**DIRECTOR**
KYLE DUNLEVY

**WRITER**
MELINDA HSU

## A VISIT TO CONCORDIA

Obi-Wan and Satine travel to Mandalore's moon Concordia in search of Death Watch renegades. Obi-Wan slips away to investigate while Satine speaks with Governor Pre Vizsla, but Obi-Wan is discovered by members of Death Watch.

## A TRAITOR IS REVEALED

Shockingly, Governor Pre Vizsla reveals himself as the leader of Death Watch. Drawing his darksaber, he springs at Obi-Wan, hoping to add another Jedi to his blade's list of victims.

The Vizslas are an ancient Mandalorian clan whose members include Death Watch leaders, bounty hunters, mercenaries, and pacifist New Mandalorians.

### SATINE'S LOOK

The character design for Duchess Satine is based on Iain McCaig's concept art of Padmé created for Episode I: *The Phantom Menace.*

"That woman **TARNISHES** the very **NAME** Mandalorian. Defend her if you will."

PRE VIZSLA

# DUCHESS SATINE TRAVELS

on the *Coronet* to Coruscant with four senators she hopes to talk into joining her peace process. Obi-Wan and Anakin accompany her as bodyguards. When Anakin discovers there is a traitor on board, the Jedi must figure out which senator is seeking to dispose of Satine and bring Mandalore into the Separatist camp.

## A TRAITOR IN THE MIDST

Anakin discovers the *Coronet*'s hold contains a sinister secret: spiderlike assassin droids hidden in a crate. Anakin must find out which senator is guilty of hiding them.

**NOTABLE CHARACTERS**

Obi-Wan Kenobi

Senator Tal Merrik

Duchess Satine Kryze

Obi-Wan Kenobi protected Satine during Mandalore's civil war. Satine fell in love with Obi-Wan and her feelings for him remain strong.

## VOYAGE OF TEMPTATION

"FEAR NOT THE FUTURE, WEEP NOT FOR THE PAST."

#40
EPISODE 13, SEASON 2

AIRDATE
FEBRUARY 5, 2010

DIRECTOR
BRIAN KALIN O'CONNELL

WRITER
PAUL DINI

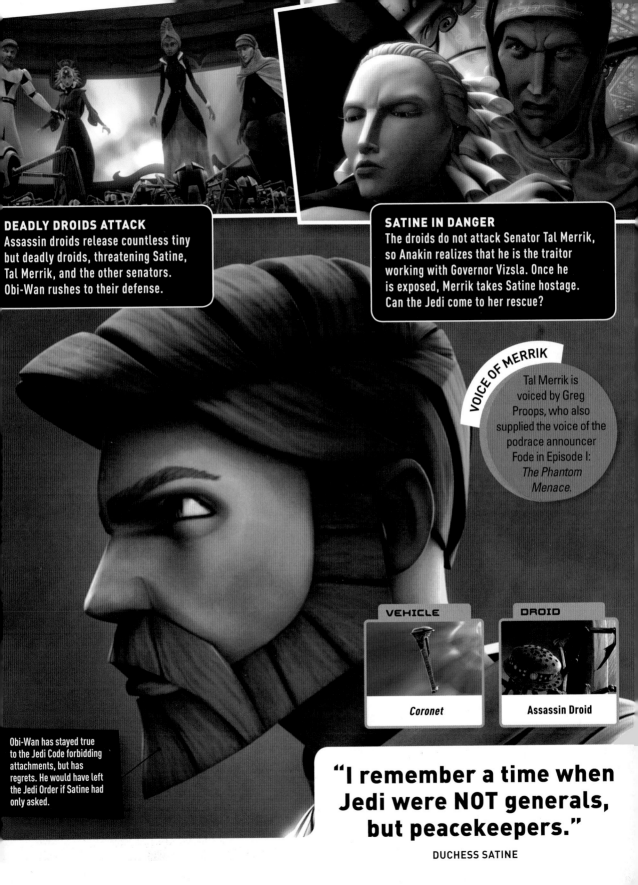

## DEADLY DROIDS ATTACK
Assassin droids release countless tiny but deadly droids, threatening Satine, Tal Merrik, and the other senators. Obi-Wan rushes to their defense.

## SATINE IN DANGER
The droids do not attack Senator Tal Merrik, so Anakin realizes that he is the traitor working with Governor Vizsla. Once he is exposed, Merrik takes Satine hostage. Can the Jedi come to her rescue?

### VOICE OF MERRIK
Tal Merrik is voiced by Greg Proops, who also supplied the voice of the podrace announcer Fode in Episode I: *The Phantom Menace.*

**VEHICLE**

*Coronet*

**DROID**

**Assassin Droid**

Obi-Wan has stayed true to the Jedi Code forbidding attachments, but has regrets. He would have left the Jedi Order if Satine had only asked.

## "I remember a time when Jedi were NOT generals, but peacekeepers."
DUCHESS SATINE

**THE REPUBLIC** prepares to invade Mandalore in response to a mysterious message from one of the planet's ministers pleading for help. Mandalore's Duchess Satine knows that no such message was sent, so she tries to discover who is concocting evidence to provoke an invasion. She reveals a plot that threatens both her life and her planet's freedom.

### EAGER FOR WAR
Death Watch leader Pre Vizsla waits for word of the Republic invasion. Once the attack begins, Death Watch will fight the Republic, posing as Mandalore's liberators and overthrowing Satine.

# DUCHESS OF MANDALORE

## "IN WAR, TRUTH IS THE FIRST CASUALTY."

**DROID**

**Cam Droid**

**OPEN AREA**

The rock formation in the plaza where Obi-Wan and Satine meet is the only part of Coruscant not covered with skyscrapers.

**VEHICLES**

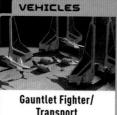

**Gauntlet Fighter/ Transport**

**Police BARC Speeder**

**Coruscant Shuttlebus**

**#41**
EPISODE 14, SEASON 2

**AIRDATE**
FEBRUARY 12, 2010

**DIRECTOR**
BRIAN KALIN O'CONNELL

**WRITER**
DREW Z. GREENBERG

## SECRET REVEALED

A brave bureaucrat named Davu Golec discovers the minister's message has been altered to sound like a plea for aid. He gives taped evidence to Satine, but to her horror, a Death Watch assassin kills Golec.

## SATINE'S SURRENDER

Satine gives Obi-Wan the tape and surrenders at the Senate building, allowing Obi-Wan to slip inside and find Padmé—who then shows the evidence to the Senate and prevents a war.

**NOTABLE CHARACTERS**

Davu Golec

Duchess Satine Kryze

Chancellor Palpatine

Cam droids are common sights on Coruscant. The police use specialized models to search for suspected criminals in the lower levels of the planet.

Members of Coruscant's upper levels often venture into its seedier districts, clad in cloaks that give them a degree of anonymity.

## "You need your FRIENDS with you, not held at arm's length."

OBI-WAN KENOBI

# AT THE BATTLE OF

Geonosis, Mace Windu killed Jango Fett. Now, aboard Admiral Kilian's ship *Endurance*, Jango's son, Boba Fett, seeks revenge. He gets his chance by infiltrating a group of clone cadets. Boba wants to destroy Mace, but is he willing to kill innocent people, too?

### NEW RECRUITS
Crasher's Clone Youth Brigade has a new member, a long-haired boy named Lucky. But Lucky is no ordinary clone cadet—his real name is Boba and he is there to attack Mace.

### KILIAN'S HONOR
Admiral Kilian is named in honor of Kilian Plunkett, lead designer for *The Clone Wars* television series.

# DEATH TRAP

**"WHO MY FATHER WAS MATTERS LESS THAN MY MEMORY OF HIM."**

### NOTABLE CHARACTERS

**Boba Fett (AKA Lucky)**

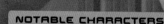

**Clone Cadet Jax**

**Admiral Kilian**

**Sergeant Crasher**

**#42**
EPISODE 20, SEASON 2

**AIRDATE**
APRIL 23, 2010

**DIRECTOR**
STEWARD LEE

**WRITER**
DOUG PETRIE

## BOBA'S REVENGE
Boba tries to eliminate Mace using a bomb. When this fails, he sabotages the *Endurance*'s reactor, sending the ship on a one-way trip to the planet Vanqor below.

## AURRA SING TAKES CONTROL
Boba and the cadets escape the doomed *Endurance* in a pod. A strange ship comes to their aid. It is *Slave I*, piloted by the bounty hunter Aurra Sing. Aurra gives Boba a harsh order: Eliminate the other cadets!

Air escapes through the hull breach that opens as the *Endurance* begins to break up.

Admiral Kilian's stubborn refusal to abandon his ship risks his demise in deep space.

# "You're NOT my brother!"
BOBA FETT

**AFTER ADMIRAL** Kilian's ship, the *Endurance*, crashes, Anakin and Mace search for survivors. But a trap set by Boba Fett explodes, and they become trapped in the ship's wreckage. Anakin sends R2-D2 for help, but the bounty hunters who are holding the *Endurance* crew hostage, give chase.

## IT'S A TRAP!
On the bridge, Anakin spots a Mandalorian helmet. Mace warns him not to touch it, but the warning comes too late—Fett's trap has been sprung and a bomb explodes!

### VEHICLE

*Slave I*

The *Endurance* crashed into Vanqor belly-first, but the warship's tough construction left its bridge intact.

# ARTOO COME HOME

**"ADVERSITY IS A FRIENDSHIP'S TRUEST TEST."**

### NOTABLE CHARACTERS

**Boba Fett**

**Aurra Sing**

**R2-D2**

**Castas**

**Bossk**

**LIGHTING THE WAY**
*Slave I* dates back to Episode V: *The Empire Strikes Back*. The ship takes off and lands on its back, and its cockpit rotates so its crew always find themselves sitting upright.

**#43**
EPISODE 21, SEASON 2

**AIRDATE**
APRIL 30, 2010

**DIRECTOR**
GIANCARLO VOLPE

**WRITER**
EOGHAN MAHONY

**ON THE TRAIL**
Seeing the explosion, Boba and the bounty hunters Aurra Sing and Castas race to find out if their trap has killed the Jedi, leaving Bossk with the captives.

**R2 TO THE RESCUE**
R2-D2 races for Anakin's starfighter and tries to get help for the trapped Jedi. But as he lifts off, Boba's ship *Slave I* is right on his tail!

**LAST SEEN**

We last saw Jango Fett's helmet in Boba's hands near the end of Episode II: *Attack of the Clones.*

R2 scans his surroundings nervously and with good reason: Vanqor is home to savage gundarks.

### "I don't WANT to take hostages—I want Windu DEAD!"

BOBA FETT

**AURRA SING** and Boba Fett threaten to kill their hostages if Mace Windu does not face Boba and give him the chance to avenge his father. Jedi Master Plo Koon and Ahsoka hunt Aurra and Boba down, following a trail of evidence from Coruscant's underworld to Hondo Ohnaka's base on Florrum, where the bounty hunters Aurra, Boba, and Bossk are waiting.

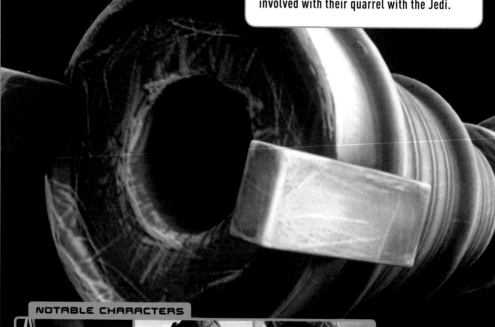

### HONDO'S HELP
Seeking a place to hide, Aurra brings Boba to Hondo's base on Florrum. The wary pirate allows them to stay, but vows not to get involved with their quarrel with the Jedi.

# LETHAL TRACKDOWN

## "REVENGE IS A CONFESSION OF PAIN."

### NOTABLE CHARACTERS

**Boba Fett**

**Jedi Master Plo Koon**

**Ahsoka Tano**

**Hondo Ohnaka**

**Aurra Sing**

### SPECIES

**Massiff**

#44
EPISODE 22, SEASON 2

**AIRDATE**
APRIL 30, 2010

**DIRECTOR**
DAVE FILONI

**WRITERS**
DAVE FILONI AND
DREW Z. GREENBER

## DEADLOCK

When Plo and Ahsoka catch up with the bounty hunters, Boba pulls a gun on Plo, and Ahsoka puts her lightsaber to Aurra's neck. Aurra blasts her way out and leaves Boba behind.

## BOBA UNDER PRESSURE

Boba is stunned by Aurra's desertion. Plo implores him to reveal where the hostages are, and Hondo says that this is what Boba's father would have wanted. What will Boba do?

### VEHICLES

**Jedi Turbo Speeder**

**Hover Taxi**

Aurra has a Rhen-Orm biocomputer implanted in her skull, allowing her to eavesdrop on faraway conversations and to investigate potential targets' identities.

**A REAL HUTTIE!**

In this episode, Aurra and Boba visit a Coruscant nightclub, where there is a pin-up of a Hutt.

Aurra's weapons of choice are her DX-13 blaster pistols, notable for their unusual dual triggers.

## "We ARE justice."

PLO KOON

# CORRUPTION

## "THE CHALLENGE OF HOPE IS TO OVERCOME CORRUPTION."

**WAR HAS CUT OFF** trade routes to Mandalore, leading to widespread smuggling and corruption. The Mandalore leader, Duchess Satine, turns to Padmé for assistance in navigating these perils. When Padmé visits the neutral world, she and Satine discover smugglers are selling tea diluted with poison in order to boost their profits. Together they set out to uncover the source of the corruption.

### A SHOCKING DISCOVERY
Having visited a school where many of the children are sick, Satine discovers that tea shipped to the school is contaminated with a toxin known as slabin. The tea is being brought to Mandalore by Moogan smugglers.

### FAMILIAR SHAPES
Look carefully in this episode and you will see shapes from Mandalorian armor used in the planet's architecture.

Satine and Padmé wear everyday clothes for informal travels around Mandalore's capital city of Sundari.

| | #45 EPISODE 5, SEASON 3 | AIRDATE OCTOBER 8, 2010 | DIRECTOR GIANCARLO VOLPE | WRITER CAMERON LITVACK |
|---|---|---|---|---|

## HIGH-LEVEL CORRUPTION

On further investigation, Satine finds high levels of corruption everywhere: from the school superintendent to Siddiq, a shipping-company employee who admits that he bribes officials.

## PADMÉ TAKES ACTION

Siddiq's information leads Satine and Padmé to the docks, where they catch the smugglers diluting the tea with slabin. Can Padmé and the guards bring them to justice?

**NOTABLE CHARACTERS**

Duchess Satine Kryze

Padmé Amidala

Siddiq

**VEHICLES**

Moogan Freight Gunship

Mandalorian Police Speeder

Naboo Royal Cruiser

Datapads are used throughout the galaxy for communications, research, record-keeping, and entertainment.

## "The MOST dangerous weapon in the galaxy is MONEY."

DUCHESS SATINE

## PADMÉ SENDS AHSOKA

to Mandalore to fight against corruption by teaching the next generation of Mandalorians about honest government. Inspired by Ahsoka's lessons, several cadets attempt to investigate the planet's food shortages—and stumble across a plot to overthrow Duchess Satine. Little do they know how high up Mandalore's goverment the plot goes.

**CADET UNIFORMS**

The chevrons on the cadets' uniforms look similar to a piece of armor on Jango and Boba Fett's breastplates.

**EVIDENCE OF CORRUPTION**
The cadets sneak off to a warehouse and discover smugglers meeting members of the Mandalorian police. Alarmed, they report their findings to Prime Minister Almec.

Ahsoka is without her lightsaber. After Obi-Wan's run-in with the Death Watch on the planet, off-worlders are no longer allowed to carry weapons on Mandalore.

The idealistic, brave Korkie Kryze is Satine's nephew, and one of the potential future leaders of Mandalore.

**#46**
EPISODE 6, SEASON 3

**AIRDATE**
OCTOBER 15, 2010

**DIRECTOR**
GIANCARLO VOLPE

**WRITER**
CAMERON LITVACK

## A DISTURBING DISCOVERY

Almec arranges to meet the cadets, but sends the police to detain them instead. When Ahsoka comes to their rescue, they quickly figure out that Almec is not what he seems—he is plotting to overthrow Satine!

## SAVING SATINE

Almec moves swiftly, arresting Satine and trying to force her into signing a phony confession of treason. It is up to Ahsoka and the cadets to overpower Almec and save the duchess.

### MANDALORIAN ABC

The Mandalorian alphabet was developed for displays aboard *Slave I* in Episode II: *Attack of the Clones.*

### NOTABLE CHARACTERS

Ahsoka Tano

Korkie Kryze

Prime Minister Almec

Amis

Lagos

Soniee

## "Lasting CHANGE can ONLY come from within."

AHSOKA TANO

# AHSOKA HAS RECURRING

visions of bounty hunter Aurra Sing attempting to assassinate Padmé. She accompanies Padmé to a conference on Alderaan and discovers that Sing is alive—and is indeed trying to kill the Naboo senator. But Ahsoka's visions have only shown her only what may happen—not how to stop the assassin.

**AHSOKA'S VISION**
Ahsoka's first visions are frustratingly vague: Aurra Sing is alive and up to no good. Later visions have a chilling clarity: Senator Amidala is the assassin's target.

## ASSASSIN

### "THE FUTURE HAS MANY PATHS—CHOOSE WISELY."

### NOTABLE CHARACTERS

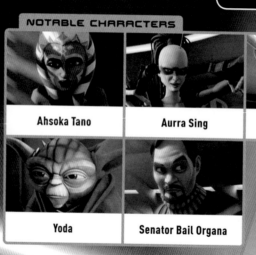

| Ahsoka Tano | Aurra Sing | Padmé Amidala |
| Yoda | Senator Bail Organa | |

**AURRA SING'S EYES**

The black stripe across Aurra Sing's eyes is an homage to the look of Daryl Hannah's character Pris in the 1982 movie *Blade Runner*.

**#47**
EPISODE 7, SEASON 3

**AIRDATE**
OCTOBER 22, 2010

**DIRECTOR**
KYLE DUNLEVY

**WRITER**
KATIE LUCAS

## PADMÉ WOUNDED

Aurra outmaneuvers Ahsoka and fires at Padmé, but the Padawan is able to use the Force to throw off her aim, turning a kill shot into a mere shoulder wound.

## AHSOKA DEFENDS PADMÉ

Ahsoka devises a plan to use a droid as a decoy for Padmé. But Aurra sees through the ruse, leading to a final confrontation between the Padawan and the bounty hunter.

Aurra uses a variety of rifles for missions that require her skills as a sniper. Later, Rako Hardeen also uses this same model of weapon.

**LOCATION**

Alderaan

**YODA'S ADVICE**

Like Ahsoka, Anakin Skywalker visits Master Yoda's quarters in Episode III: *Revenge of the Sith* to discuss troubling premonitions.

There are many rumors about Aurra Sing's origins, and she has used a number of aliases, including Nashtah and Shatta Aunuanna.

## "To SEE clearly, more experience YOU need."

YODA

## ANAKIN AND OBI-WAN

lead the Republic forces defending the planet of Kamino, home of the cloning facilities. General Grievous's mission is to destroy as many clones as he can and halt the production of new ones, while Asajj Ventress aims to steal the original clone DNA sample of Jango Fett.

### RETURN TO KAMINO
Returning with the 501st Legion to defend their home planet, Kamino, Echo and Fives reunite with their old friend, maintenance clone 99.

## ARC TROOPERS

"FIGHTING A WAR TESTS A SOLDIER'S SKILLS, DEFENDING HIS HOME TESTS A SOLDIER'S HEART."

### HOMAGE TO HEVY
Fives and Echo wear decals saying "FOR HEVY" in Aurebesh, paying respect to their comrade who sacrificed his life in the episode "Rookies."

Climate change drowned Kamino's continents long ago. The Kaminoans now dwell in clusters of towers that rise above the waves on stilts.

**DROID**

Aqua Droid

**SPECIES**

Aiwha

**NOTABLE CHARACTERS**

Obi-Wan Kenobi

Asajj Ventress

General Grievous

Echo

**#48**
EPISODE 2, SEASON 3

**AIRDATE**
SEPTEMBER 17, 2010

**DIRECTOR**
KYLE DUNLEVY

**WRITER**
CAMERON LITVACK

104

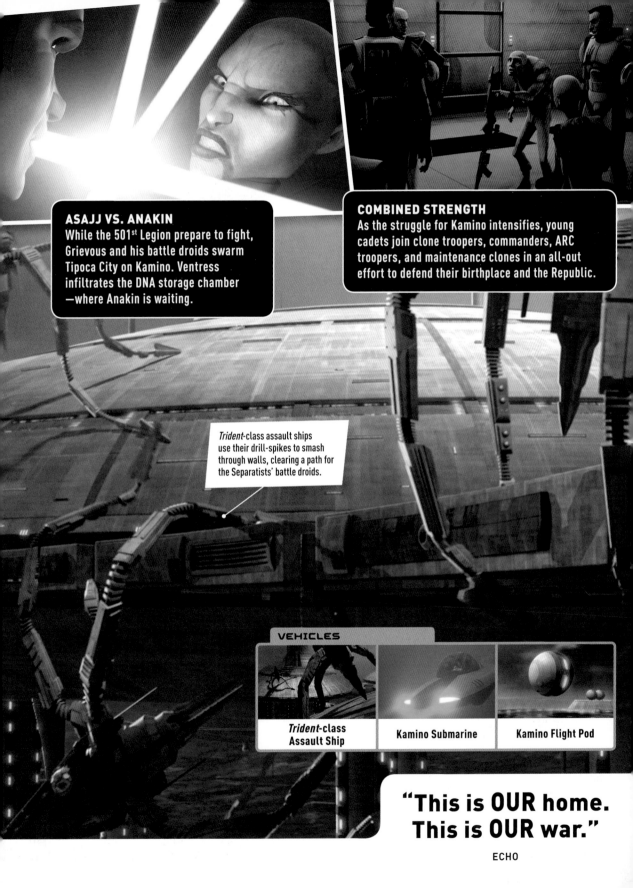

## ASAJJ VS. ANAKIN

While the 501st Legion prepare to fight, Grievous and his battle droids swarm Tipoca City on Kamino. Ventress infiltrates the DNA storage chamber —where Anakin is waiting.

## COMBINED STRENGTH

As the struggle for Kamino intensifies, young cadets join clone troopers, commanders, ARC troopers, and maintenance clones in an all-out effort to defend their birthplace and the Republic.

*Trident*-class assault ships use their drill-spikes to smash through walls, clearing a path for the Separatists' battle droids.

### VEHICLES

*Trident*-class Assault Ship

Kamino Submarine

Kamino Flight Pod

## "This is OUR home. This is OUR war."

ECHO

# THE TRADE FEDERATION

has blockaded Pantora in an effort to bully Chairman Papanoida into joining the Separatists. After Papanoida's two daughters are kidnapped, he and his son Ion follow the evidence to Tatooine and the galactic underworld while Ahsoka and Senator Riyo Chuchi hunt for clues aboard a Trade Federation ship above Pantora.

## PRESSURE ON PAPANOIDA

On Coruscant, Chairman Papanoida works to en the Separatist blockade of his homeworld of Pa When he refuses to join Dooku's cause, crimin kidnap his daughters Chi Eekway and Che Ama

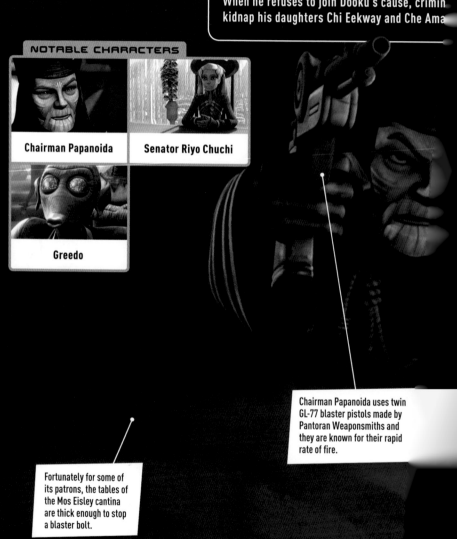

### NOTABLE CHARACTERS

Chairman Papanoida

Senator Riyo Chuchi

Greedo

Chairman Papanoida uses twin GL-77 blaster pistols made by Pantoran Weaponsmiths and they are known for their rapid rate of fire.

Fortunately for some of its patrons, the tables of the Mos Eisley cantina are thick enough to stop a blaster bolt.

# SPHERE OF INFLUENCE

"A CHILD STOLEN IS A LOST HOPE."

**#49**
EPISODE 4, SEASON 3

**AIRDATE**
OCTOBER 1, 2010

**DIRECTOR**
KYLE DUNLEVY

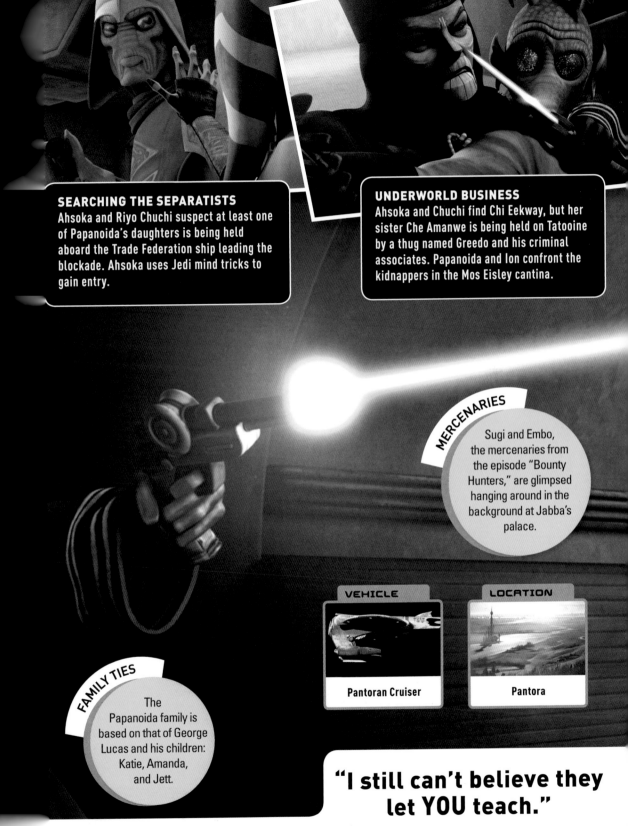

## SEARCHING THE SEPARATISTS
Ahsoka and Riyo Chuchi suspect at least one of Papanoida's daughters is being held aboard the Trade Federation ship leading the blockade. Ahsoka uses Jedi mind tricks to gain entry.

## UNDERWORLD BUSINESS
Ahsoka and Chuchi find Chi Eekway, but her sister Che Amanwe is being held on Tatooine by a thug named Greedo and his criminal associates. Papanoida and Ion confront the kidnappers in the Mos Eisley cantina.

### MERCENARIES
Sugi and Embo, the mercenaries from the episode "Bounty Hunters," are glimpsed hanging around in the background at Jabba's palace.

### VEHICLE
Pantoran Cruiser

### LOCATION
Pantora

### FAMILY TIES
The Papanoida family is based on that of George Lucas and his children: Katie, Amanda, and Jett.

## "I still can't believe they let YOU teach."
PADMÉ AMIDALA

**AN APPARENTLY** innocent shopping trip to Coruscant turns sinister when Cad Bane abducts C-3PO and R2-D2. Bane is seeking information they may know about the Senate building and its security protocols— information that will allow the ruthless bounty hunter to do a job for one of his shadowy clients.

## MADE TO TALK

While R2-D2 enjoys the comforts of a spa, C-3PO is captured and taken to Cad Bane. The bounty hunter ransacks the protocol droid's memory in a futile search for information about the Senate building.

**FAMOUS LINE**

Todo 360's parting line "Thanks for the memories" was a hit song in 1938 and Bob Hope's signature number.

Todo 360 really hates being treated like a butler: He's a techno-service droid, if you please. What's a techno-service droid? A butler, basically. Sorry, Todo.

# EVIL PLANS

## "A FAILURE IN PLANNING IS A PLAN FOR FAILURE."

**NOTABLE CHARACTERS**

Cad Bane

C-3PO

R2-D2

**#50**
EPISODE 8, SEASON 3

**AIRDATE**
NOVEMBER 5, 2010

**DIRECTOR**
BRIAN KALIN
O'CONNELL

**WRITERS**
STEVE MITCHELL AN
CRAIG VAN SICKL

## 2'S CHOICE

[B]ane's droids hunt down R2-D2, but he is [d]efiant and refuses to release the information. [M]echanical thugs threaten to dismantle C-3PO [h]owever, so R2-D2 is forced to surrender.

## THANKS FOR THE MEMORIES

After extracting the information he needs from R2-D2, Bane orders the droids dumped on the street. Their disturbing experience has been wiped from their memories.

### DROIDS

| | |
|---|---|
| Baker Droid | Spa Droid |
| Shopkeeper Droid | Protocol Droid |

These Jogan fruits will serve as a garnish atop a fruit cake, the favorite dessert of Senator Aang, the Roonan guest of honor at Padmé's party.

## "I'm your WORST nightmare, pal!"

CAD BANE

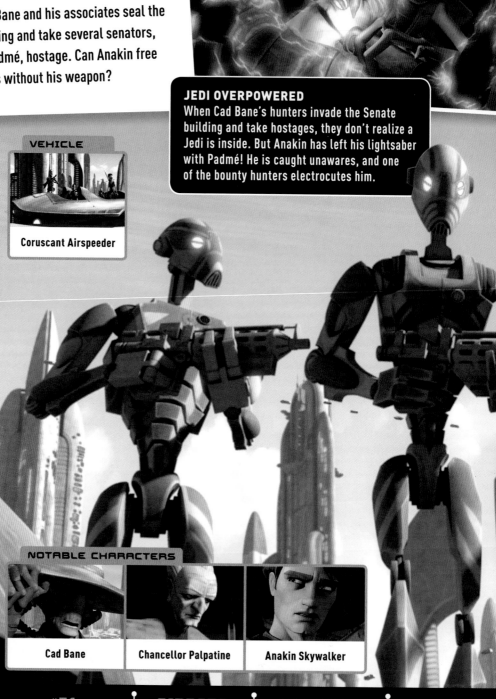

# ANAKIN SNEAKS INTO

the Senate building on Coruscant to meet Padmé. To prove his trust in her, he hands her his lightsaber. Meanwhile, in a surprise attack, Cad Bane and his associates seal the Senate building and take several senators, including Padmé, hostage. Can Anakin free the hostages without his weapon?

## JEDI OVERPOWERED

When Cad Bane's hunters invade the Senate building and take hostages, they don't realize a Jedi is inside. But Anakin has left his lightsaber with Padmé! He is caught unawares, and one of the bounty hunters electrocutes him.

**VEHICLE**

Coruscant Airspeeder

## HOSTAGE CRISIS

"A SECRET SHARED IS A TRUST FORMED."

### NOTABLE CHARACTERS

Cad Bane

Chancellor Palpatine

Anakin Skywalker

| #51 EPISODE 22, SEASON 1 | AIRDATE MARCH 20, 2009 | DIRECTOR GIANCARLO VOLPE | WRITER EOGHAN MAHONY |

## BANE'S DEMANDS
With a Jedi and senators as his hostages, Bane has plenty of bargaining power. Bane informs Chancellor Palpatine of his demands: The Republic must free Ziro the Hutt from prison.

## A DIFFICULT SITUATION
The Republic releases Ziro. Bane surrounds the hostages with bombs, warning that he will detonate them if anyone tries to interfere with his hunters while they escape with Ziro. Can Anakin stop them?

One of the galaxy's most feared bounty hunters and mercenaries, the amoral Cad Bane will take on any mission, provided the job pays enough credits.

### TWO VOICES
Voice actor Corey Burton supplies the very different voices of Cad Bane and Ziro the Hutt.

One of Bane's hirelings is Shahan Alama, a Weequay bounty hunter with a mechanical arm recycled from a combat droid.

### IMPORTANT HOSTAGES
Among the senators held hostage are Riyo Chuchi of Pantora and Onaconda Farr of Rodia.

### DROIDS
BD-3000 Luxury Droid

IG-86 Sentinel Droid

## "I got BUSINESS with the SENATE. How about you fellas step aside?"
CAD BANE

**YEARS AGO,** Ziro the Hutt hid a journal detailing the criminal activities of the five Hutt families. Fearing Ziro might tell the Republic their secrets, the Hutts broke him out of prison and locked him up themselves. When old flame Sy Snootles helps Ziro escape, the Hutts send Cad Bane after him—but the Jedi are also on his tail. Who will reach him first and can Ziro trust Sy?

## ODD COUPLE
The arrogant Jedi Quinlan Vos joins Obi-Wan on Ziro's trail. The quest will take this odd couple from Coruscant to Nal Hutta and Teth, quarreling all the while.

## LAST WORDS
Ziro's dying line is, "What a world, what a world"—the same words said by the Wicked Witch of the West as she disintegrates in the 1939 movie *The Wizard of Oz*.

# HUNT FOR ZIRO

## "LOVE COMES IN ALL SHAPES AND SIZES."

The vocal stylings of the Pa'lowick chanteuse Sy Snootles have entertained audiences everywhere from the heights of Coruscant to the depths of Hutt Space.

## NOTABLE CHARACTERS

**Ziro The Hutt**

**Sy Snootles**

**Jedi Master Quinlan Vos**

**Cad Bane**

**#52**
**EPISODE 9, SERIES 3**

**AIRDATE**
**NOVEMBER 12, 2010**

**DIRECTOR**
**STEWARD LEE**

**WRITERS**
**STEVE MITCHELL AN**
**CRAIG VAN SICKLE**

112

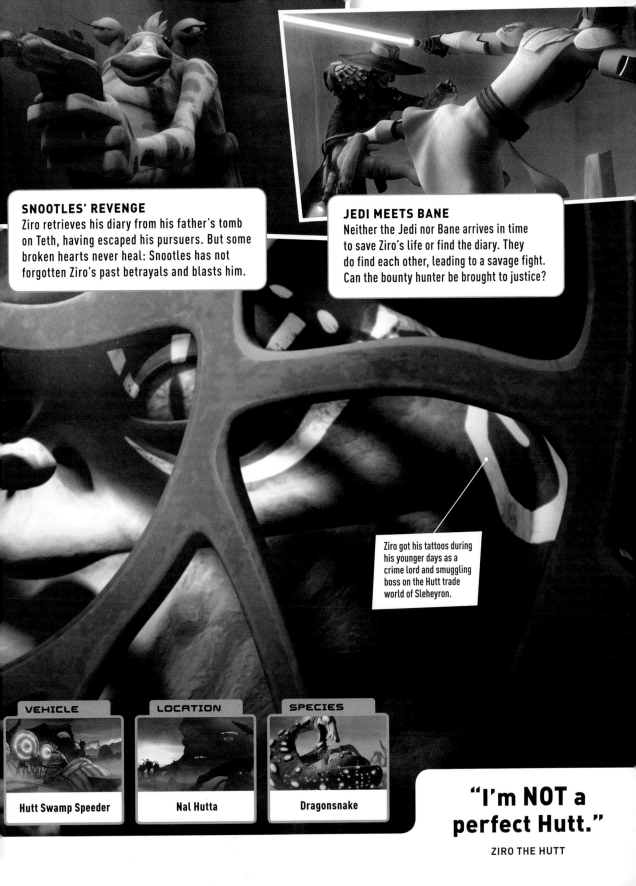

## SNOOTLES' REVENGE
Ziro retrieves his diary from his father's tomb on Teth, having escaped his pursuers. But some broken hearts never heal: Snootles has not forgotten Ziro's past betrayals and blasts him.

## JEDI MEETS BANE
Neither the Jedi nor Bane arrives in time to save Ziro's life or find the diary. They do find each other, leading to a savage fight. Can the bounty hunter be brought to justice?

Ziro got his tattoos during his younger days as a crime lord and smuggling boss on the Hutt trade world of Sleheyron.

**VEHICLE**
Hutt Swamp Speeder

**LOCATION**
Nal Hutta

**SPECIES**
Dragonsnake

# "I'm NOT a perfect Hutt."
ZIRO THE HUTT

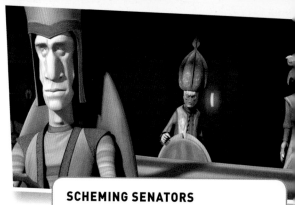

**AHSOKA TRAVELS** with Padmé to the Separatist capital, Raxus, where she discovers that some of the Republic's enemies are in fact decent people with forthright political beliefs. They discuss negotiations for peace, but shadowy forces on both sides of the war are determined to wreck any chance of peace in order to prolong the war for their own financial profit.

### SCHEMING SENATORS
Banking representative Nix Card and Senators Lott Dod and Gume Saam meet to engineer a Separatist attack on Coruscant and derail a Senate vote on the war.

## HEROES ON BOTH SIDES

*"FEAR IS A GREAT MOTIVATOR."*

### CHANGING STYLE
The heroes of the Clone Wars—most notably Ahsoka Tano—wear new outfits in this episode, reflecting the passage of time since the beginning of the series.

Raxus Secundus, often just called Raxus, is a lush world. It is in the same system as Raxus Prime, a despoiled industrial world covered with meters of ancient junk.

### NOTABLE CHARACTERS

**Padmé Amidala**

**Senator Mina Bonteri**

**Lux Bonteri**

**Ahsoka Tano**

### LOCATION

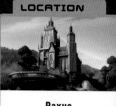

**Raxus**

**#53**
EPISODE 10, SEASON 3

**AIRDATE**
NOVEMBER 19, 2010

**DIRECTOR**
KYLE DUNLEVY

**WRITER**
DANIEL ARKIN

114

**SEPARATIST SENATOR**
Padmé meets with her old friend Mina Bonteri, now a Separatist senator. They work for negotiations that could end the fighting, unaware of the impending attack.

**DROIDS INVADE POWER ROOM**
General Grievous sends demolition droids to infiltrate a key complex of generators supplying power to Coruscant. The attack causes a massive blackout, frightening the Senate into continuing the war effort.

**GUME SAAB**
The Ishi Tib Senator Gume Saam can also be seen behind Palpatine at the end of Episode II: *Attack of the Clones*.

Mina Bonteri's son, Lux, still mourns the death of his father, who was killed by clone troopers in a battle on Aargonar.

**DROID**

Demolition Droid

**VEHICLE**

Gozanti Cruiser

**"In THIS case, our business is VIOLENCE."**

LOTT DOD

**COUNT DOOKU** abandons peace negotiations with the Republic, but Padmé refuses to give up hope. She joins Senators Bail Organa and Onaconda Farr in an effort to stop a bill that would create new clones, prolonging the war and stretching the Republic's finances. But the would-be peacemakers are pursued by thugs who want to intimidate them.

## DOOKU REJECTS PEACE

Dooku announces that his supporter, Senator Mina Bonteri, has been killed by Republic troops and withdraws the Separatist peace proposal. Stunned, Padmé vows to keep working to end the war.

# PURSUIT OF PEACE

## "TRUTH CAN STRIKE DOWN THE SPECTER OF FEAR."

Q-2 blaster pistols are light and easy to conceal, but still pack a punch.

### NOTABLE CHARACTERS

**Padmé Amidala**

**Teckla Minnau**

**Senator Bail Organa**

### NABOO RETREAT

Padmé's handmaiden Teckla serves dinner at the Naboo lakeside retreat in Episode II: *Attack of the Clones*.

### VEHICLES

**Coruscant Police Speeder**

**Viper Speeder Bike**

**#54**
EPISODE 11, SEASON 3

**AIRDATE**
DECEMBER 3, 2010

**DIRECTOR**
DUWAYNE DUNHAM

**WRITER**
DANIEL ARKIN

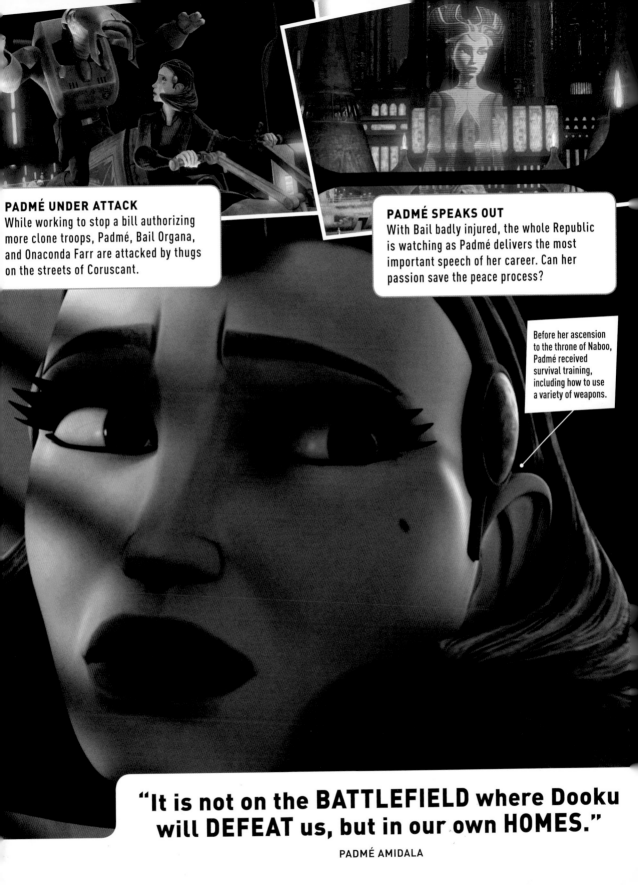

## PADMÉ UNDER ATTACK
While working to stop a bill authorizing more clone troops, Padmé, Bail Organa, and Onaconda Farr are attacked by thugs on the streets of Coruscant.

## PADMÉ SPEAKS OUT
With Bail badly injured, the whole Republic is watching as Padmé delivers the most important speech of her career. Can her passion save the peace process?

Before her ascension to the throne of Naboo, Padmé received survival training, including how to use a variety of weapons.

# "It is not on the BATTLEFIELD where Dooku will DEFEAT us, but in our own HOMES."
PADMÉ AMIDALA

## PADMÉ AND HER ALLIES

try to persuade the Senate to cut military spending in a bid to end the war. This action pits them against the Republic's pro-military faction who accuses them of being unpatriotic. Things take a dark turn when one of Padmé's allies is murdered. She and Senator Bail Organa set out to find out who killed Senator Onaconda Farr.

### A FRUSTRATED DETECTIVE
Detective Tan Divo searches for Farr's killer, but is frustrated when Padmé and Bail interfere. Divo believes that Padmé should focus on being a senator while he concentrates on the investigation.

### SENATE REGALIA
In this episode Padmé wears an elaborate headdress for Senate business and ceremonial occasions.

Lolo Purs is a representative assisting the planet's senator and her mentor, Onaconda Farr, with legislative business.

# SENATE MURDERS

"SEARCHING FOR THE TRUTH IS EASY. ACCEPTING THE TRUTH IS HARD."

### NOTABLE CHARACTERS

**Padmé Amidala**

**Detective Tan Divo**

**Lolo Purs**

**Senator Onaconda Farr**

**Senator Bail Organa**

**Senator Mon Mothma**

#55
EPISODE 15, SEASON 2

AIRDATE
MARCH 19, 2010

DIRECTOR
BRIAN KALIN
O'CONNELL

WRITER
DREW Z. GREENBERG

**SUSPECT IDENTIFIED**
Divo discovers Farr was given a Kaminoan poison that only affects Rodians. That points to Kaminoan Senator Halle Burtoni—whom Lolo Purs also claims attacked her in the Senate building corridor.

**LOLO'S MISTAKE**
Padmé realizes that Lolo Purs wasn't affected by the poison because she did not drink her wine—so it was Lolo who poisoned the drinks! Lolo realizes she has been caught and turns on Padmé.

**"I'll handle the INSPECTING and you can stick to the SENATING."**

DETECTIVE TAN DIVO

## DARTH SIDIOUS ORDERS

Count Dooku to eliminate his apprentice, the Nightsister Asajj Ventress, as a test of his loyalty. Thanks only to Dooku's negligence, Ventress survives and flees to the planet Dathomir, where her kin care for her. She plots with the Nightsisters' matriarch, Mother Talzin, to take revenge on Dooku.

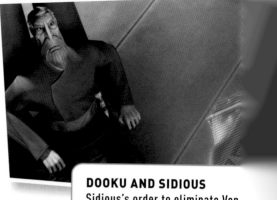

### DOOKU AND SIDIOUS
Sidious's order to eliminate Ven angers Dooku: She is one of his effective agents. But Dooku wil challenge his master, and must

# NIGHTSISTERS

## "THE SWIFTEST PATH TO DESTRUCTION IS THROUGH VENGEANCE."

### NOTABLE CHARACTERS

| Asajj Ventress | Mother Talzin | Count Dooku |

### VEHICLE

Fanblade Starfighter

### LOCATION

Dathomir

**FANBLADE**
Ventress's fighter is known as a Fanblade. The design made its debut in the *Clone Wars* micro-series in 2003.

As a Sith, Dooku has shed a life' worth of Jedi teachings that der that the Force be used with rest A Sith imposes his will upon the letting raw emotions channel its

**#56**
EPISODE 12, SEASON 3

**AIRDATE**
JANUARY 7, 2011

**DIRECTOR**
GIANCARLO VOLPE

**W**
KAT

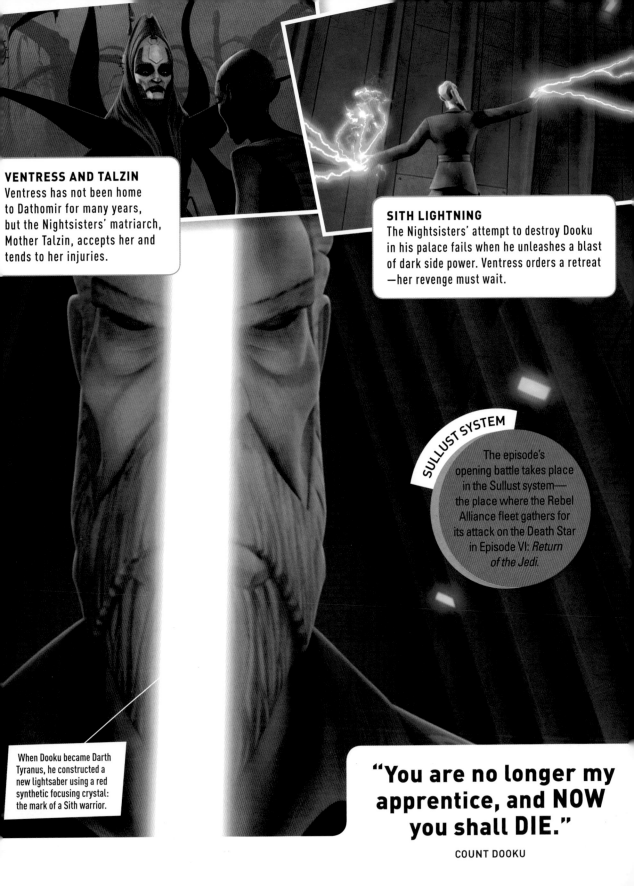

**VENTRESS AND TALZIN**
Ventress has not been home to Dathomir for many years, but the Nightsisters' matriarch, Mother Talzin, accepts her and tends to her injuries.

**SITH LIGHTNING**
The Nightsisters' attempt to destroy Dooku in his palace fails when he unleashes a blast of dark side power. Ventress orders a retreat —her revenge must wait.

**SULLUST SYSTEM**
The episode's opening battle takes place in the Sullust system— the place where the Rebel Alliance fleet gathers for its attack on the Death Star in Episode VI: *Return of the Jedi.*

When Dooku became Darth Tyranus, he constructed a new lightsaber using a red synthetic focusing crystal: the mark of a Sith warrior.

**"You are no longer my apprentice, and NOW you shall DIE."**

COUNT DOOKU

# CONVINCED THAT JEDI

assassins are stalking him, Count Dooku asks Mother Talzin to bring him a new apprentice to replace Ventress. The Nightsisters plot to find a Nightbrother from the same village that produced Darth Maul. They intend to give the warrior to Dooku, while ensuring his real loyalty is to them. Dooku tests his new warrior with great success.

## A DEADLY GAME

To find a suitable candidate for Dooku's apprentice, Asajj tests the Nightbrothers. She faces their best warriors in brutal combat until only one remains: Savage Opress.

## MONSTER

### "EVIL IS NOT BORN, IT IS TAUGHT."

Besides being a huge weapon with a wickedly sharp blade, Savage's ax was forged with the Nightsisters' most potent magic.

### SLAIN JEDI

The Jedi Master slain at the end of this episode is a member of the Roonan species. His name—not heard until the next episode —is Halsey.

**#57**
EPISODE 13, SEASON 3

**AIRDATE**
JANUARY 14, 2011

**DIRECTOR**
KYLE DUNLEVY

**WRITER**
KATIE LUCAS

## SAVAGE TRANSFORMATION
Mother Talzin's sorcery transforms Savage into a gigantic warrior, rippling with muscle and the energies of the dark side of the Force. He is ready for presentation to Dooku.

## INTO BATTLE
To test his new apprentice, Dooku sends Savage to Devaron. There, Savage strides into a battle between Separatist droids and Republic clones, eager to strike down his first Jedi.

Dooku offers Talzin an alliance with the Separatists, but she rejects it: The Nightsisters have always followed their own path.

### DOOKU'S SHIP
The ship piloted by Dooku (and later by Opress) is a Solar Sailer. It is first seen in Episode II: *Attack of the Clones*, where it is flown by an FA-4 pilot droid.

### NOTABLE CHARACTERS

**Asajj Ventress**

**Savage Opress**

**Count Dooku**

**VEHICLE**

**Nightsister Speeder**

**LOCATION**

**Devaron**

## "Count DOOKU, may I present Savage OPRESS?"
MOTHER TALZIN

## ANAKIN AND OBI-WAN

hunt for the culprit who slaughtered Jedi on Devaron. They find out it was Savage Opress, the dark warrior created by the Nightsisters and trained by Count Dooku. Dooku, Asajj Ventress, and the Jedi all seek to make Savage their pawn, but the hulking Nightbrother has his own plans for his future.

### DOOKU OVERCOMES SAVAGE

Dooku trains Savage ruthlessly in the ways of the dark side before sending him to kidnap Toydaria's King Katuunko, whose betrayal of the Separatists has not been forgotten.

### DOOKU'S FATE

Dooku holds his lightsabers like scissors at his apprentice's throat, foreshadowing his own fate in Episode III: *Revenge of the Sith.*

# WITCHES OF THE MIST

## "THE PATH TO EVIL MAY BRING GREAT POWER, BUT NOT LOYALTY."

The curved hilt of Dooku's lightsaber gives him precise control of the blade; in combat the Sith Lord relies on finesse and speed, not raw strength.

| | #58 EPISODE 14, SEASON 3 | AIRDATE JANUARY 21, 2011 | DIRECTOR GIANCARLO VOLPE | WRITER KATIE LUCAS |

**ASAJJ AND SAVAGE ADVANCE**
After he kills rather than captures Katuunko, Savage joins Asajj against Dooku. But they cannot overpower him and are forced to flee.

**SAVAGE'S VISION**
Escaping from all those who seek to use him, Savage returns to Mother Talzin. She gives him a new quest: to search out his mysterious brother, still alive somewhere in the Outer Rim.

**LOCATION**

Serenno

**VEHICLE**

*Thief's Eye*

**NOTABLE CHARACTERS**

Asajj Ventress

Obi-Wan Kenobi

Savage Opress

Ventress's twin sabers can be joined together to create a single, double-bladed saberstaff.

**"Your ANGER is your STRENGTH."**

COUNT DOOKU

# A MYSTERIOUS FORCE

draws Anakin, Obi-Wan, and Ahsoka to a planet ruled by a trio of supremely powerful Force-users. For eons, the Father has kept the balance between his Daughter and Son, who embody the light and dark sides of the Force. Now, he wants Anakin to take over the task as the long-prophesied Chosen One.

## THE LIGHT SIDE
After landing on Mortis, the Jedi first meet the Daughter, who embodies the light side of the Force and can assume the form of a glowing griffin.

The Jedi experience strange visions on Mortis: Obi-Wan communes with the spirit of Qui-Gon Jinn, while the Son assumes the form of Anakin's mother, Shmi.

## OVERLORDS

"BALANCE IS FOUND IN THE ONE WHO FACES HIS GUILT."

### FAMILIAR VOICES
Actors Liam Neeson and Pernilla August returned to voice the spirits of Qui-Gon Jinn and Shmi Skywalker for this episode.

**#59**
EPISODE 15, SEASON 3

**AIRDATE**
JANUARY 28, 2011

**DIRECTOR**
STEWARD LEE

**WRITER**
CHRISTIAN TAYLOR

## THE DARK SIDE
Opposing the Daughter is the Son, who commands the dark side and can take many forms. Testing Anakin's power, the Daughter grabs Obi-Wan, while the Son seizes Ahsoka.

## THE CHOSEN ONE
Anakin passes the test by overcoming both the Daughter and the Son and freeing his friends. The Father declares he is indeed the Chosen One, destined to replace him and keep his children in balance. But will Anakin agree?

Mortis is an ever-changing realm, described as a conduit through which the Force flows, acting as both an amplifier and a magnet for it.

### SPECIES

| Gargoyle | Griffin |

### LOCATION

Mortis

### NOTABLE CHARACTERS

| Anakin Skywalker | Father | Ahsoka Tano |

| Jedi Master Qui-Gon Jinn | Shmi Skywalker |

### NEW INSIGHTS
The Mortis trilogy was written in close consultation with George Lucas, who offered significant new insights into the nature of the Force and the Jedi prophecy of the Chosen One.

## "If he is the CHOSEN ONE, he will discover it here."

QUI-GON JINN

**ANAKIN HAS REFUSED**

to assume the Father's burden, so the balance between the Daughter and the Son tips, with both disobeying the Father and seeking to overcome the other. The Son takes Ahsoka captive and infects her with the dark side, while the Daughter enlists Obi-Wan to help stop her brother.

## LETHAL WEAPON
The Daughter leads Obi-Wan to the Altar of Mortis, where he retrieves a dagger that the Daughter says will give him power over the Son.

# ALTAR OF MORTIS

"HE WHO SURRENDERS HOPE, SURRENDERS LIFE."

**FORCEFUL VOICES**

Sam Witwer and Adrienne Wilkinson, the voices of Son and Daughter, played Starkiller and Maris Brood in the videogame *Star Wars: The Force Unleashed*.

### VEHICLE

**Eta-class Shuttle**

Forced to fight his own Padawan, Anakin duels defensively, trying to merely deflect Ahsoka's blows.

### NOTABLE CHARACTERS

**Obi-Wan Kenobi**

**Son**

**Daughter**

**#60**
EPISODE 16, SEASON 3

**AIRDATE**
FEBRUARY 4, 2011

**DIRECTOR**
BRIAN KALIN O'CONNELL

**WRITER**
CHRISTIAN TAYLOR

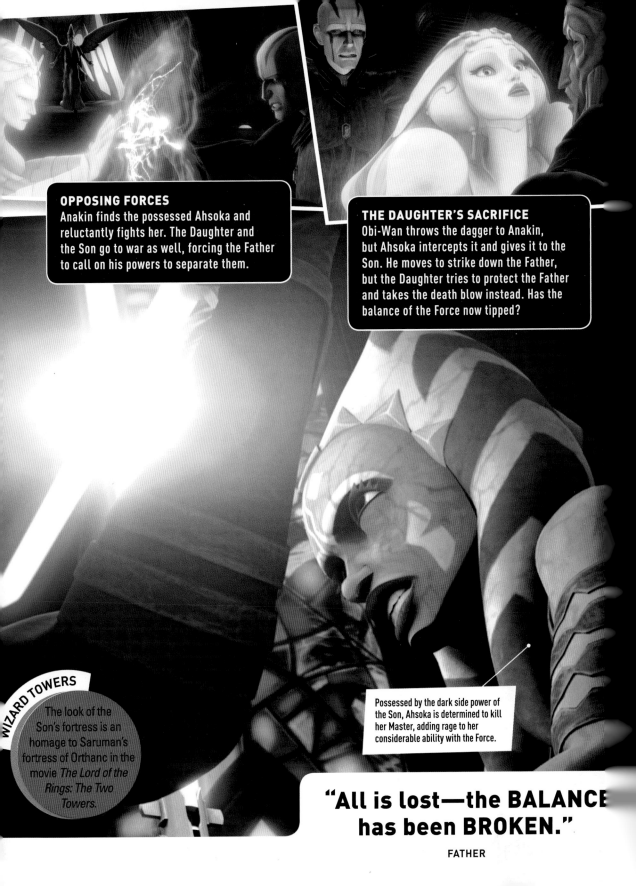

**OPPOSING FORCES**
Anakin finds the possessed Ahsoka and reluctantly fights her. The Daughter and the Son go to war as well, forcing the Father to call on his powers to separate them.

**THE DAUGHTER'S SACRIFICE**
Obi-Wan throws the dagger to Anakin, but Ahsoka intercepts it and gives it to the Son. He moves to strike down the Father, but the Daughter tries to protect the Father and takes the death blow instead. Has the balance of the Force now tipped?

**WIZARD TOWERS**
The look of the Son's fortress is an homage to Saruman's fortress of Orthanc in the movie *The Lord of the Rings: The Two Towers*.

Possessed by the dark side power of the Son, Ahsoka is determined to kill her Master, adding rage to her considerable ability with the Force.

**"All is lost—the BALANCE has been BROKEN."**
FATHER

**ON MORTIS**, the Son seeks to convert Anakin to the dark side by showing him a terrifying vision of his future—a destiny the Son promises he can help prevent from happening. Declaring that the Son has done the forbidden by ending his sister's life, the Father makes a fateful decision to intervene in order to restore balance to the Force.

**THE FATHER'S ADVICE**

With the Daughter dead, the Force has fallen out of balance on Mortis. Anakin does not know what to do, and the Father tells him to seek counsel with the Force.

**SPEEDER CONCEPT**

The Jedi jumpspeeder is based on early concept art of the speeder bikes that appear in Episode VI: *Return of the Jedi*.

**PREMONITION**

Anakin's vision includes events that come to pass in Episode III: *Revenge of the Sith* and Episode IV: *A New Hope*.

# GHOSTS OF MORTIS

**"HE WHO SEEKS TO CONTROL FATE SHALL NEVER FIND PEACE."**

**VEHICLE**

Jedi Jumpspeeder

**NOTABLE CHARACTERS**

Anakin Skywalker

Father

Son

**#61**
EPISODE 17, SEASON 3

**AIRDATE**
FEBRUARY 11, 2011

**DIRECTOR**
STEWARD LEE

**WRITER**
CHRISTIAN TAYLC

130

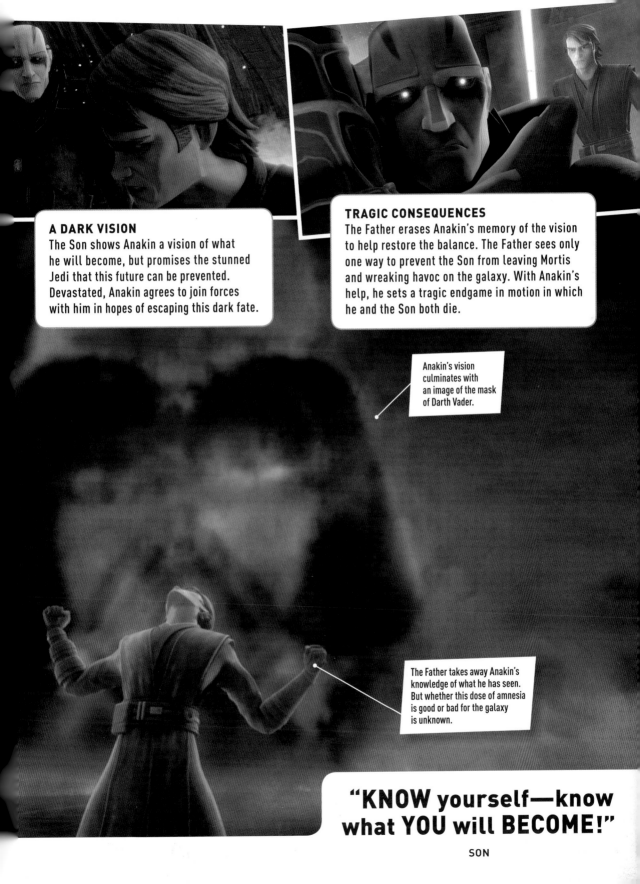

## A DARK VISION
The Son shows Anakin a vision of what he will become, but promises the stunned Jedi that this future can be prevented. Devastated, Anakin agrees to join forces with him in hopes of escaping this dark fate.

## TRAGIC CONSEQUENCES
The Father erases Anakin's memory of the vision to help restore the balance. The Father sees only one way to prevent the Son from leaving Mortis and wreaking havoc on the galaxy. With Anakin's help, he sets a tragic endgame in motion in which he and the Son both die.

Anakin's vision culminates with an image of the mask of Darth Vader.

The Father takes away Anakin's knowledge of what he has seen. But whether this dose of amnesia is good or bad for the galaxy is unknown.

## "KNOW yourself—know what YOU will BECOME!"

SON

# JEDI MASTER EVEN PIELL

has been imprisoned by the Separatists in the Citadel: a notorious prison on the planet Lola Sayu. Anakin, Obi-Wan, and a squad of clones are sent to rescue Piell before he is forced to reveal the coordinates of the Nexus Route: a secret path through hyperspace that could change the course of the war.

## DROIDS IN CHARGE
Ships arriving on Lola Sayu are scanned for life-forms, so the shuttle carrying the Jedi is piloted by a squad of reprogrammed battle droids under R2-D2's command. The Jedi and clones hibernate in carbon freeze so they cannot be detected.

**SIMILAR SPEECH**

Osi Sobeck's speech patterns are similar to actor Christopher Walken's, whom Lucas considered for the part of Han Solo in Episode IV: *A New Hope*.

# THE CITADEL

## "ADAPTATION IS THE KEY TO SURVIVAL."

Ahsoka has disobeyed her master's orders and joined the rescue mission. She learned such disobedience from Anakin himself.

**#62**
EPISODE 18, SEASON 3

**AIRDATE**
FEBRUARY 14, 2011

**DIRECTOR**
KYLE DUNLEVY

**WRITER**
MATT MICHNOVETZ

## CITADEL BREAK-IN
When the Jedi come out of hibernation, they face a harrowing climb up a cliff face to the Citadel entrance. They finally gain access, but the prison's warden, Osi Sobeck, discovers them and sends out swarms of droid attackers.

## DOUBLE RESCUE
The team finally reaches Piell, but he informs them that they must also rescue Captain Tarkin, who has the other half of the coordinates. Before they can reach Tarkin, the Jedi face dangerous traps such as an electrified grid that nearly fries Anakin.

Concerned for Ahsoka's safety, Anakin told her to stay behind. Ahsoka claims Plo Koon ordered her to join the mission after Anakin went into carbon freeze, but this isn't true.

**LOCATION**

Lola Sayu

**DROID**

Pilot Battle Droid

**NOTABLE CHARACTERS**

Osi Sobeck

Captain Tarkin

### PLAYING BALL
Tactical droid K2-B4 is an homage to the NBA's Los Angeles Lakers. The droid's purple-and-yellow body and name are a nod to superstar Kobe Bryant, who wears No. 24.

## "You're going to be my GUESTS for a very LONG time."
OSI SOBECK

**AFTER FREEING** Even Piell and Captain Tarkin from the Citadel prison, Anakin and Obi-Wan attempt to return to Coruscant. But the fortress's warden, Osi Sobeck, is determined to prevent them from escaping. Many perils lie between the Jedi and freedom. The Jedi split into two separate groups in an attempt to evade Separatist forces.

## A DROID TO THE RESCUE
Sobeck captures Obi-Wan's group and sends them away to be interrogated. But their guards are intercepted by battle droids led by a familiar astromech—R2-D2 to the rescue!

# COUNTERATTACK

"ANYTHING THAT CAN GO WRONG WILL."

### NOTABLE CHARACTERS

| R2-D2 | Echo | Captain Tarkin |
|-------|------|----------------|

| #63 EPISODE 19, SEASON 3 | AIRDATE MARCH 4, 2011 | DIRECTOR BRIAN KALIN O'CONNELL | WRITER MATT MICHNOVETZ |
|---|---|---|---|

## AGREEING ON A STRATEGY
Meanwhile, Anakin, Ahsoka, and Captain Tarkin make a perilous trip through a fuel line. Anakin and Tarkin discover they agree about how the Jedi might wage war more effectively.

## UNDER ATTACK
The two groups meet at the landing field—but Sobeck has flooded the area with his droid troops. ARC Trooper Echo is an unlucky victim of their fire. Can the Jedi escape?

In close quarters Ahsoka sometimes switches to a Shien variant combat style, in which she wields her lightsaber using a reverse grip.

B2 battle droids are the brutes of the Separatist Army; they are not very intelligent, but they are well-armed and difficult to take down.

**THIRD TARKIN**
Voice actor Stephen Stanton is the third to play Captain Tarkin. Peter Cushing did the honors in Episode IV: *A New Hope*, while Wayne Pygram had a cameo in Episode III: *Revenge of the Sith*.

**DROID**

Security Battle Droid

**VEHICLE**

STAP

## "FIND them, commander. Get the information. And KILL them all."
OSI SOBECK

## SAVAGE, WOLF-LIKE

beasts called anoobas pursue Anakin, Ahsoka, Even Piell, and Captain Tarkin across the prison world Lola Sayu. The Jedi are trying to return to Coruscant with the secret coordinates for a crucial hyperspace route. Jedi Master Plo Koon prepares a task force to rescue them, but will it arrive in time?

### VICIOUS ATTACK

Warden Osi Sobeck releases savage anoobas to hunt the Jedi and stop them from escaping. One of the beasts mauls Jedi Master Even Piell. With his last bit of strength, Piell tells Ahsoka the Nexus Route coordinates.

## CITADEL RESCUE

### "WITHOUT HONOR, VICTORY IS HOLLOW."

**SPECIES**

Anoobas

**VEHICLES**

Droid Tri-Fighter

**NOTABLE CHARACTERS**

Jedi Master Plo Koon

Jedi Master Even Piell

Osi Sobeck

**#64**
EPISODE 20, SEASON 3

**AIRDATE**
MARCH 11, 2011

**DIRECTOR**
STEWARD LEE

**WRITER**
MATT MICHNOVETZ

**HELP ON ITS WAY**
A Republic fleet arrives at Lola Sayu and battles its Separatist defenders. Jedi Master Saesee Tiin leads the fighters, while Plo Koon's gunships prepare for a surface assault.

**TARGETING TARKIN**
Sobeck believes the only way to keep the Nexus Route a secret is to end Republic Captain Tarkin's life but Ahsoka stops him just in time.

**ANOOBA ART**
Anoobas first appeared in Terryl Whitlach's concept art for Episode I: *The Phantom Menace.*

Plo Koon's Wolfpack, led by the Jedi Master and Commander Wolffe, are experts at difficult extractions under fire.

Clone troopers are trained to board gunships at a run, grabbing on and giving the all-clear in mere seconds (a stationary target has a short life expectancy).

"If we aren't **WILLING** to do what it takes to win, we risk **LOSING** everything we try to **PROTECT.**"

ANAKIN SKYWALKER

# PADAWAN LOST

## "WITHOUT HUMILITY, COURAGE IS A DANGEROUS GAME."

## AHSOKA IS CAPTURED

by Trandoshans and taken to their moon Wasskah, where a party of Trandoshans led by Garnac has organized a cruel game. The group releases its prisoners and hunts them down for sport. Ahsoka joins a band of dispirited Jedi younglings, who are also being hunted, in a battle for survival.

### ON THE RUN

The Trandoshans dump Ahsoka and the other captives on Wasskah's beach, then open fire. Those who survive have until morning before the hunt begins. Overnight, Ahsoka teams up with other Jedi younglings who are also fugitives.

### SNIVVIAN HOMAGE

One of the fugitives, Snivvian Katt Mol, has an outfit that plays homage to that worn by Snaggletooth, a 1978 Kenner action figure from Episode IV: *A New Hope*.

The fugitive younglings mostly move at night, as the Trandoshans prefer to hunt Wasskah's luckless refugees during the day.

#65
EPISODE 21, SEASON 3

AIRDATE
APRIL 1, 2011

DIRECTOR
DAVE FILONI

WRITER
BONNIE MARK

**HOVERING HUNTERS**
The hunters close in on the fugitives on open speeders equipped with blasters for targeting prey on the ground. Ahsoka and most of the younglings escape: Kalifa tries to put up a fight, but she isn't so lucky.

**WISE ENCOURAGEMENT**
Ahsoka tries to rally the younglings, urging them to reclaim their Jedi training. Rather than live like hunted animals, they will need to figure out how to strike back at the hunters.

Practice and Jedi reflexes enable the younglings to run along branches as if they were the decks of starships.

**NOTABLE CHARACTERS**

| Kalifa | O-Mer | Garnac |
| --- | --- | --- |

**LOCATION**

Wasskah

**VEHICLES**

| Hunt Ship | Hover Pod |
| --- | --- |

## "The sun has risen—let the HUNT begin!"

GARNAC

**AHSOKA AND HER** comrades remain under attack from Trandoshan hunters on Wasskah when they meet an unexpected new ally—Chewbacca the Wookiee, who is also being hunted. Chewie finds enough parts to make a communicator that can transmit a distress signal, but the Trandoshans are closing in....

## AHSOKA'S PLAN
Chewie cobbles together a transmitter and calls for help from other Wookiees. Meanwhile, the younglings plot to steal Pteropter hover pods and attack the Trandoshans' aerial hunting lodge.

# WOOKIEE HUNT

"A GREAT STUDENT IS WHAT THE TEACHER HOPES TO BE."

### CRYSTAL SKULL
There is a crystal skull in the Trandoshan hunting lodge that wouldn't look out of place in the movie *Indiana Jones and the Kingdom of the Crystal Skull.*

### SUGI'S SHIP
A side of the *Halo* is emblazoned with art of a Tooka doll holding a knife. The Aurebesh letters say "NICE PLAYING WITH YA."

**NOTABLE CHARACTERS**

Chewbacca

Garnac

**LOCATION**

Hunting Lodge

**VEHICLE**

*Halo*

**#66**
EPISODE 22, SEASON 3

**AIRDATE**
APRIL 1, 2011

**DIRECTOR**
DAVE FILONI

**WRITER**
BONNIE MARK

**HUNTING THE HUNTERS**
The fugitives capture one of the Trandoshans and use the Force to hypnotize him into calling for help. When the hunters respond, the fugitives seize their hover pods.

**WOOKIEE RESCUE**
Amid the Trandoshans's gunfire, the *Halo* descends. The Trandoshans dive for cover as Wookiees fire rifles from above. Chewie's reinforcements have arrived!

Chewbacca is bright and technologically skilled so he can make a transmitter using parts found in the wreckage of the crashed transport.

Wookiees are known for their great strength and violent tempers, but also for their skill with machinery and technical abilities.

# "We'll do it the WOOKIEE way... "

JINX

THE MON CALAMARI and the Quarren share the waterworld of Mon Cala, but relations between the two are close to breaking point following the murder of the Mon Calamari King, Kolina. The Republic sends troops to defend the Mon Calamari, but face a Separatist attack by Karkarodon warlord Riff Tamson, who intends to destroy Prince Lee-Char, son of the dead king.

## GROWING TENSION
As relations between the Mon Calamari and Quarren worsen, Senator Meena Tills meets with Captain Ackbar to command him to protect Prince Lee-Char.

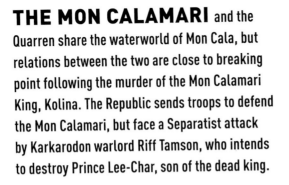

## WATER WAR

"WHEN DESTINY CALLS, THE CHOSEN HAVE NO CHOICE."

### WHAT'S IN A NAME?
Prince Lee-Char's name is a reversal of "Charlie." Some fans will know Charlie the Tuna as the mascot for the US brand of StarKist tuna.

### NOTABLE CHARACTERS

**Anakin Skywalker**

**Captain Ackbar**

**Prince Lee-Char**

**Riff Tamson**

Mon Calamari spear blasters are dual-purpose weapons useful at long range and at close quarters.

**#67**
EPISODE 1, SEASON 4

**AIRDATE**
SEPTEMBER 16, 2011

**DIRECTOR**
DUWAYNE DUNHAM

**WRITER**
JOSE MOLINA

## PURSUIT OF THE PRINCE
While Separatist aqua droids and Republic clone troopers square off, Riff Tamson swims after Lee-Char, hoping to end the prince's life with one well-aimed bite.

## RETALIATION
The Republic holds the line in the initial assault, but the Separatists strike back with strange new weapons: massive cybernetic jellyfish. The fight for Mon Cala is on!

Ackbar is the head of the Mon Calamari Guard and chief military advisor to Mon Cala's royal family.

**VEHICLE**

Devilfish Sub

**LOCATION**

Mon Cala

**WISE WARNING**

Ackbar's warning that "It's an attack" is a variation on his much-loved line from Episode VI: *Return of the Jedi*— "It's a trap!"

## "Your FATHER would be PROUD of you."

CAPTAIN ACKBAR

# THE SEPARATISTS

tighten their grip on the ocean world Mon Cala. The Jedi continue to protect the Mon Calamari leadership while Riff Tamson moves to enslave the planet's people under orders from his master, Count Dooku. In desperation, the Jedi turn to Naboo's Gungans for help....

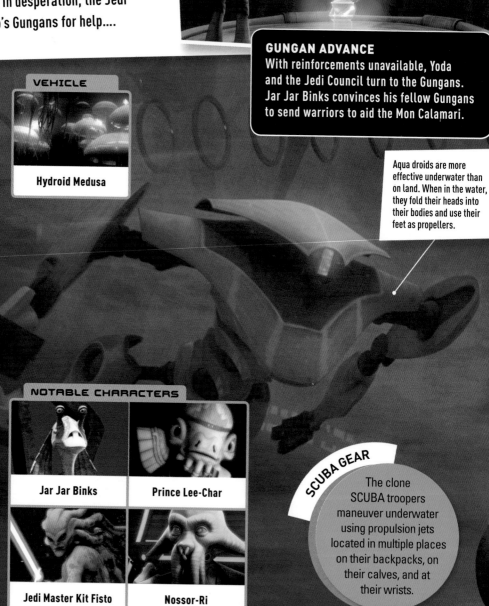

## GUNGAN ADVANCE

With reinforcements unavailable, Yoda and the Jedi Council turn to the Gungans. Jar Jar Binks convinces his fellow Gungans to send warriors to aid the Mon Calamari.

Aqua droids are more effective underwater than on land. When in the water, they fold their heads into their bodies and use their feet as propellers.

## GUNGAN ATTACK

"ONLY THROUGH FIRE IS A STRONG SWORD FORGED."

### VEHICLE

**Hydroid Medusa**

### NOTABLE CHARACTERS

**Jar Jar Binks**

**Prince Lee-Char**

**Jedi Master Kit Fisto**

**Nossor-Ri**

### SCUBA GEAR

The clone SCUBA troopers maneuver underwater using propulsion jets located in multiple places on their backpacks, on their calves, and at their wrists.

| #68 EPISODE 2, SEASON 4 | AIRDATE SEPTEMBER 16, 2011 | DIRECTOR BRIAN KALIN O'CONNELL | WRITER JOSE MOLINA |

## A CALL TO ACTION

Prince Lee-Char of Mon Calamari rallies his people, who are being held captive by Riff Tamson. He tells them that soon they will be free. Meanwhile, the Gungans arrive to help their cause.

## SEPARATISTS STRIKE BACK

Enraged by Lee-Char's defiance and Gungan interference, Riff Tamson sends *Trident* drilling gunships to churn up deadly vortices in which no army can operate. Ahsoka and Prince Lee-Char only just get away.

### A SIGN OF HOPE

The Mon Calamari are technologically advanced, but sometimes the ancient ways are best: Prince Lee-Char calls his people by blowing on a conch shell.

Anakin altered his saber to function underwater. Aquatic Jedi such as Kit Fisto use special lightsabers that are waterproof at all times.

## "HOPE is something we cannot allow our ENEMY to possess."

COUNT DOOKU

# ANAKIN AND KIT FISTO

are held by Riff Tamson as the battle for Mon Cala continues. Ahsoka and Prince Lee-Char make a plan to liberate Tamson's prison camp, while Riff Tamson tortures the Jedi hostages. The Karkarodon warlord wants to know where the prince is so that he can destroy him and set himself up as Mon Cala's ruler.

## UNDER INTERROGATION
Determined to find Lee-Char and eliminate him, Tamson brutally interrogates Anakin, Kit Fisto, Padmé, and Jar Jar. He is eager to see who will break first.

## A SHARK'S TALE
The demise of Riff Tamson is an homage to another movie with a shark villain—the 1975 blockbuster *Jaws*.

Riff proudly wears the insignia of the Separatists. He hopes his planet's alliance with Dooku will make Karkaris a galactic power.

**PRISONERS**

"CROWNS ARE INHERITED, KINGDOMS ARE EARNED."

### SPECIES

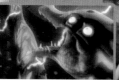

Electric Eel

### NOTABLE CHARACTERS

Padmé Amidala

Riff Tamson

Jar Jar Binks

**#69**
EPISODE 3, SEASON 4

**AIRDATE**
SEPTEMBER 23, 2011

**DIRECTOR**
DANNY KELLER

**WRITER**
JOSE MOLINA

## LEE-CHAR'S RISKY PLAN

Lee-Char allows himself to be captured. He hopes his bravery in facing Riff Tamson will inspire the Mon Calamari captives to rise up. He also hopes the Quarren, who also live on Mon Cala, will reconsider their alliance with the Separatists.

## A LAST CHANCE

Tamson orders the prince's execution. But the Quarren finally decide to join forces with the Mon Calamari and free Lee-Char. In a dramatic confrontation, the prince proves himself by defeating Tamson once and for all.

### ACKBAR'S BATON

Admiral Ackbar's 1983 action figure came with the battle baton seen in this episode. Like many children of that era, director Danny Keller re-imagined the baton as a weapon.

Karkarodons have teeth like razors, but the real damage is done by their enormously strong jaws.

## "There's PLENTY of SUFFERING to go around!"

RIFF TAMSON

# PADMÉ AND ANAKIN

visit Naboo to investigate rumors that the Gungans plan to fight with General Grievous and the Separatists. They find that a Gungan minister, Rish Loo, is tricking his people into joining the Separatists on orders from Count Dooku. Anakin must find a way to stop the Gungans from swapping sides.

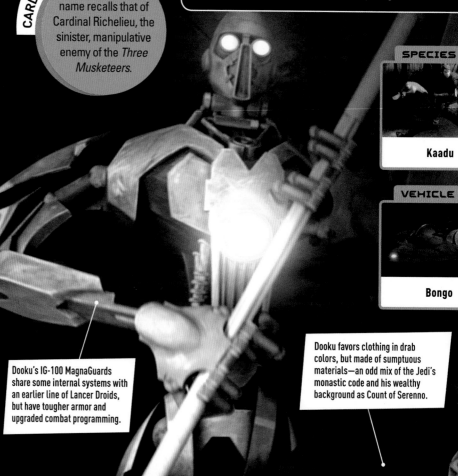

## DROID ATTACK

Padmé and Anakin discover Rish Loo has hypnotized the Gungan leader, Boss Lyonie. When his treachery is uncovered, Loo sends commando droids to eliminate Anakin and Padmé, and to cover his escape, but they fail. Once Lyonie has recovered, he resumes his friendship with the Naboo people and vows not to fight against them.

### CARDINAL RICHELIEU

Rish Loo's name recalls that of Cardinal Richelieu, the sinister, manipulative enemy of the *Three Musketeers*.

## SHADOW WARRIOR

**"WHO A PERSON TRULY IS CANNOT BE SEEN WITH THE EYE."**

**SPECIES**

Kaadu

**VEHICLE**

Bongo

Dooku's IG-100 MagnaGuards share some internal systems with an earlier line of Lancer Droids, but have tougher armor and upgraded combat programming.

Dooku favors clothing in drab colors, but made of sumptuous materials—an odd mix of the Jedi's monastic code and his wealthy background as Count of Serenno.

**#70**
EPISODE 4, SEASON 4

**AIRDATE**
SEPTEMBER 30, 2011

**DIRECTOR**
BRIAN KALIN O'CONNELL

**WRITER**
DANIEL ARKIN

**GRIEVOUS FACE-OFF**
When Grievous arrives to lead the Gungan army, he finds the tables have turned. He is captured by the very forces he hoped to use as allies against the Naboo.

**ANAKIN CAPTURED**
Meanwhile, Dooku captures Anakin and then offers to exchange him for General Grievous. Padmé has a difficult choice to make: keep Grievous and win the war or free Anakin.

**MOVIE HOMAGE**
The title of this episode is the English translation of *Kagemusha*, a 1982 movie directed by the legendary Akira Kurosawa and executive produced by George Lucas.

**NOTABLE CHARACTERS**

Anakin Skywalker

General Grievous

Minister Rish Loo

Boss Lyonie

**"The Sith control EVERYTHING. You just don't KNOW it."**

COUNT DOOKU

**C-3PO AND R2-D2** have been brought to help clone troopers deliver relief supplies to the planet Aleen, which has been devastated by quakes. They tumble through a breach in the planet's surface into a strange underworld, where they learn that the fracture between the two worlds must be sealed to stop the quakes and restore balance.

### STRANGE UNDERWORLD
After falling into the caverns beneath Aleen, the droids encounter the treelike Kindalo, who complain that foul air from the surface is poisoning them.

### A NEW HELMET
Wolffe's helmet was redesigned for this episode to look sim[ilar] to the one worn by Commander Neyo in Episode III: *Revenge of the Sith.*

Formally known as CC-3636, Commander Wolffe is a battle-hardened veteran with scars and a cybernetic eye—the result of a close encounter with Asajj Ventress.

# MERCY MISSION

## "UNDERSTANDING IS HONORING THE TRUTH BENEATH THE SURFACE."

### NOTABLE CHARACTERS

| C-3PO | R2-D2 | Commander Wolffe | Orphne |
|-------|-------|------------------|--------|

| #71 EPISODE 5, SEASON 4 | AIRDATE OCTOBER 7, 2011 | DIRECTOR DANNY KELLER | WRITER BONNIE MARK |
|---|---|---|---|

## FILLING THE VOID
The Kindalo send the droids to meet a strange being named Orphne, whose riddles reveal that the breach between the surface and the lower world must be repaired.

## DROIDS TO THE RESCUE
Returning to the surface, C-3PO and R2-D2 work to close the seal to the underworld. It seems that only they can restore the balance on Aleen.

**LOCATION**

Aleen

C-3PO wasn't designed to be anywhere near battles, but he is relieved to think that his skills as a translator and interpreter could help Aleen's refugees.

## "Who PACKED the translator DROID?"
COMMANDER WOLFFE

# C-3PO AND R2-D2 ARE

on their way home to Coruscant from the planet Aleen when they are forced to flee a Separatist attack by commandeering a Y-wing. They crash-land on the planet Patitite Pattuna, where tiny natives capture them—and this is just the first of a series of strange adventures for the droids.

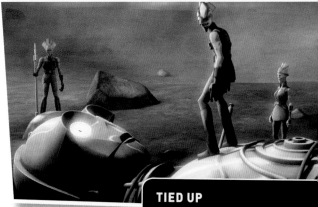

## TIED UP

The Patitites are small but overpower the droids with ion weapons that overload their circuits. But R2-D2 manages to squash their leader, Big Hay-Zu, and the droids escape.

## NOMAD DROIDS

"WHO'S THE MORE FOOLISH, THE FOOL OR THE FOOL WHO FOLLOWS HIM?"

### LOCATION

**Balnab**

### VEHICLE

*Marauder*

### NOTABLE CHARACTERS

**C-3PO**

**R2-D2**

**Big Hay-Zu**

### SPECIES

**Patitite Pattuna**

The Patitites cheer Big Hay-Zu's death, but are puzzled by C-3PO's talk about a strange phenomenon called "democracy."

A green splotch is all that's left of the Big Hay-Zu, who was Patitite Pattuna's despot until R2-D2 landed on him.

**#72**
EPISODE 6, SEASON 4

**AIRDATE**
OCTOBER 14, 2011

**DIRECTOR**
STEWARD LEE

**WRITERS**
STEVE MITCHELL AN
CRAIG VAN SICKLE

**AN AUDIENCE WITH ALBEE DEWA**
Having fled to the planet Balnab, the droids are captured again and brought before a hologram of the great ruler Albee Dewa. R2-D2 is suspicious that Balnab's ruler is not all that he seems....

**GLADIATOR DROIDS**
Having escaped the natives, the two droids are caught by pirates, who throw them in a pit to fight other droids. Will this never end?

**CLASSIC ADVENTURES**
The droids' adventures in this episode are reminiscent of two beloved classic stories—*Gulliver's Travels* and *The Wizard of Oz*.

Every galactic culture agrees that squashing a planet's ruler is a breach of etiquette. Sometimes C-3PO wishes he could have his memory erased.

**WISE WORDS**
The opening quote for this episode is from Obi-Wan Kenobi in Episode IV: *A New Hope*.

**DROIDS**

Pit Droid | ASP Droid

**"CONGRATULATIONS! You are now a democracy!"**

C-3PO

**THE 501ST LEGION,** led by Anakin, braves heavy fire to invade Umbara, a gloomy Separatist stronghold. Down there, amid shadows and fog, cunning fighters are waiting. Anakin is ordered to return to Coruscant. General Krell is put in command, but he shows little regard for Captain Rex's opinion or his troopers' lives.

## TENTACLE ATTACK

Clone troopers Tup and Hardcase soon run into an Umbaran predator—a terrifying cluster of tentacles known as a vixus. It is not the first enemy the clones will encounter.

# DARKNESS ON UMBARA

### "THE FIRST STEP TOWARD LOYALTY IS TRUST."

### SPOT THE UMBARAN

Senator Mee Deechi and Sly Moore, Palpatine's aide in the prequel movies, are Umbaran.

**LOCATION**

Umbara

| | #73<br>EPISODE 7, SEASON 4 | AIRDATE<br>OCTOBER 28, 2011 | DIRECTOR<br>STEWARD LEE | WRITER<br>MATT MICHNOVETZ |
|---|---|---|---|---|

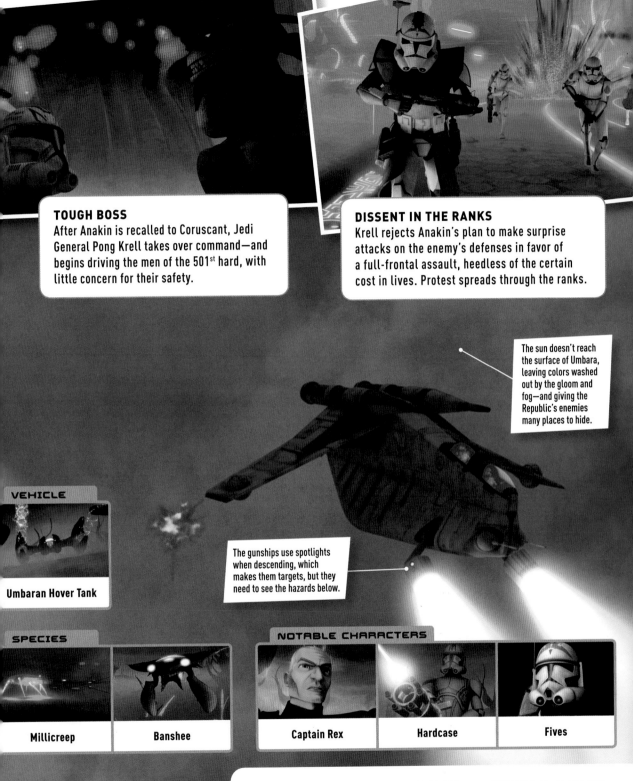

## TOUGH BOSS
After Anakin is recalled to Coruscant, Jedi General Pong Krell takes over command—and begins driving the men of the 501st hard, with little concern for their safety.

## DISSENT IN THE RANKS
Krell rejects Anakin's plan to make surprise attacks on the enemy's defenses in favor of a full-frontal assault, heedless of the certain cost in lives. Protest spreads through the ranks.

The sun doesn't reach the surface of Umbara, leaving colors washed out by the gloom and fog—and giving the Republic's enemies many places to hide.

**VEHICLE**

**Umbaran Hover Tank**

The gunships use spotlights when descending, which makes them targets, but they need to see the hazards below.

**SPECIES**

**Millicreep**

**Banshee**

**NOTABLE CHARACTERS**

**Captain Rex**

**Hardcase**

**Fives**

## "You have a SPARK of TENACITY, Captain—I'll give you that."
GENERAL KRELL

**THE INVASION** of Umbara continues, as Jedi General Krell orders his troopers to make a suicidal frontal attack on an airbase. These orders leave the clones, including Fives, on the edge of rebellion. Captain Rex must wrestle with difficult questions about where his responsibility as a clone commander lies.

## KRELL'S ORDERS

Krell insists the clones travel down a narrow gorge that will leave them dangerously exposed to enemy fire. Rex objects, but Krell responds icily that there is no time for alternatives.

**APPO MOVES UP**

One of the clone troopers, Sergeant Appo, becomes a commander and marches on the Jedi Temple with the newly christened Darth Vader in Episode III: *Revenge of the Sith*.

# THE GENERAL

## "THE PATH OF IGNORANCE IS GUIDED BY FEAR."

Tanks are piloted by a single Umbaran who occupies a cockpit in the vehicle's "head."

Umbaran crawler tanks are heavily armed: Blaster cannons protrude from the head, tail, and body segments.

## NOTABLE CHARACTERS

**Sergeant Appo**

**Fives**

**Hardcase**

**#74**
EPISODE 8, SEASON 4

**AIRDATE**
NOVEMBER 4, 2011

**DIRECTOR**
WALTER MURCH

**WRITER**
MATT MICHNOVETZ

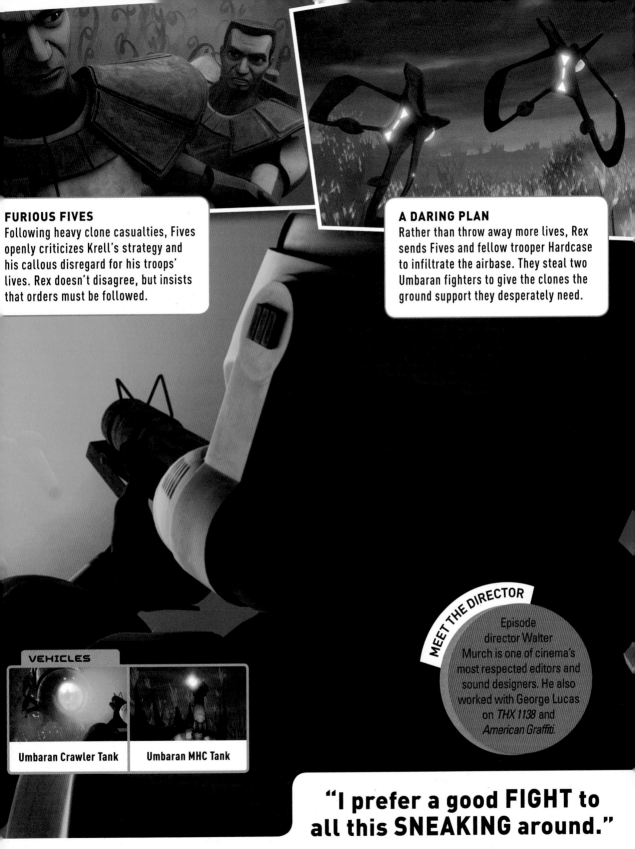

### FURIOUS FIVES
Following heavy clone casualties, Fives openly criticizes Krell's strategy and his callous disregard for his troops' lives. Rex doesn't disagree, but insists that orders must be followed.

### A DARING PLAN
Rather than throw away more lives, Rex sends Fives and fellow trooper Hardcase to infiltrate the airbase. They steal two Umbaran fighters to give the clones the ground support they desperately need.

**VEHICLES**

Umbaran Crawler Tank

Umbaran MHC Tank

**MEET THE DIRECTOR**

Episode director Walter Murch is one of cinema's most respected editors and sound designers. He also worked with George Lucas on *THX 1138* and *American Graffiti.*

# "I prefer a good FIGHT to all this SNEAKING around."

HARDCASE

## JEDI GENERAL KRELL

orders the 501st Legion to continue to the Umbaran capital, showing no concern for the casualties they are certain to take. The troops begin to argue among themselves. Fives, Jesse, and Hardcase launch a rogue mission to destroy an Umbaran supply ship from the inside.

### DEFIANT SOLDIER

Fives decides to defy Krell, infiltrating an Umbaran airbase on an unauthorized mission. Captain Rex warns the rebellious ARC trooper that he won't be able to cover for him.

### WARSHIP DESIGN

The warship seen above Umbara in this episode is a design by Ryan Church originally proposed for Episode III: *Revenge of the Sith.*

Jesse's helmet displays the Republic logo, the same logo that is tattooed on his face.

# PLAN OF DISSENT

## "THE WISE MAN LEADS, THE STRONG MAN FOLLOWS."

### NOTABLE CHARACTERS

**Fives**

**Jesse**

**Hardcase**

**#75**
EPISODE 9, SEASON 4

**AIRDATE**
NOVEMBER 11, 2011

**DIRECTOR**
KYLE DUNLEVY

**WRITER**
MATT MICHNOVETZ

## A TRAP IS SET

Fives, Jesse, and Hardcase fly their fighters into the supply ship, hoping to blow up its reactor. The ship's battle droids activate shields, however, trapping them inside.

## THE ULTIMATE SACRIFICE

Hardcase realizes the shields will stop missile fire, but won't prevent a clone from carrying a missile pod to the reactor: In order to achieve this, he has to sacrifice his life.

### NOVEL BEGINNINGS

The Z-95 Headhunters flown by the clones date back to Brian Daley's 1978 novel *Han Solo at Stars' End,* one of the earliest works in the Expanded Universe.

Jesse hasn't been trained as a pilot, yet he is a competent soldier. Thanks to advanced technology and practice, he can fly an Umbaran fighter.

### VEHICLES

**Umbaran Starfighter**

**Separatist Transport**

**Umbaran Support Ship**

## "We are part of something LARGER."

CAPTAIN REX

## JEDI GENERAL KRELL

orders Fives and Jesse to be executed for insubordination, pushing the 501st Legion to the breaking point. The clones soon discover that their ruthless commander has further plans that will harm the entire Legion. Now they must stop him and bring him to justice for his actions.

### A MUTINY

A firing squad prepares to execute Fives and Jesse, but Captain Rex makes an appeal and the clones refuse the order. They have had enough of their ruthless Jedi general.

## CARNAGE OF KRELL

**"OUR ACTIONS DEFINE OUR LEGACY."**

### NOTABLE CHARACTERS

**Captain Rex**

**Jedi General Pong Krell**

**Dogma**

### SPECIES

**Vixus**

Flip-down night-vision filters are essential on dark and gloomy Umbara.

**YOUNG AT HEART**

In this episode, Waxer's helmet is decorated with a cartoon of Numa, the Twi'lek child he met in the episode "Innocents of Ryloth."

**#76**
EPISODE 10, SEASON 4

**AIRDATE**
NOVEMBER 18, 2011

**DIRECTOR**
KYLE DUNLEVY

**WRITER**
MATT MICHNOVETZ

160

## CLONE AGAINST CLONE

Before matters can be settled, word comes of an offensive by Umbarans disguised in clone armor. To Rex's horror, the attackers turn out not to be Umbarans, but fellow clones.

## KRELL IS BROUGHT TO ACCOUNT

Rex figures out that Krell deliberately sent some of their brothers into combat against them, knowing that clones are trained to follow orders blindly. Rex decides to arrest Krell, even though as a Jedi, he will be a formidable opponent.

Rex's helmet is custom-built, combining elements of new and old helmet designs used by the clone troopers.

## "What I'm proposing is highly TREASONOUS."

CAPTAIN REX

**ZYGERRIAN SLAVERS** led by Darts D'Nar have invaded the planet of Kiros. Republic forces respond to the Separatist attack. On exploring the colony, however, they find no residents—just battle droids. They fear the inhabitants are in the hands of slavers. Moreover, the commander of the invasion force has wired the planet's capital with deadly bombs.

## OBI-WAN'S CHALLENGE
The Zygerrian commander Darts D'Nar has planted bombs around the city. Obi-Wan challenges D'Nar to combat. If he loses, he will become Dooku's prisoner.

# KIDNAPPED

## "WHERE WE ARE GOING ALWAYS REFLECTS WHERE WE CAME FROM."

### SPECIES

| | |
|---|---|
| Blixus | Convor Bird |

### LOCATION

Kiros

TECORA

The name of the Zygerrian slave ship, the *Tecora*, is als the name of a real-wo 19th-century slave ship.

**#77**
EPISODE 11, SERIES 4

**AIRDATE**
NOVEMBER 25, 2011

**DIRECTOR**
KYLE DUNLEVY

**WRITERS**
HENRY GILROY WI
STEVEN MELCHIN

162

## DEMOLITION SQUAD
Meanwhile, Anakin and Ahsoka race around the city, battling droids and defusing bombs to make it safe. Obi-Wan continues to distract D'Nar, then manages a tactical retreat.

## DANGEROUS GUARDIAN
Anakin and Ahsoka leap aboard the *Tecora*, D'Nar's ship, in a bid to capture the Zygerrian commander. But a fearsome guardian, the blixus, lurks in the hold.

### NOTABLE CHARACTERS

**Anakin Skywalker**

**Ahsoka Tano**

**Darts D'Nar**

### DROID

**Sniper Droideka**

### DARK EPISODES
"Kidnapped" and the two episodes that follow are an adaptation of *Slaves of the Republic*, a six-issue *Star Wars* comic-book series from Dark Horse Comics.

A blaster cannon has a very powerful recoil for a vehicle as small as a BARC speeder sidecar. The speeder pilot must work to keep the vehicle balanced.

## "Bow DOWN and surrender to me, you Jedi FILTH."
DARTS D'NAR

**HAVING DEFEATED** the blixus beast and the slave trader Darts D'Nar, the Jedi learn that Zygerrian slavers plan to sell Kiros's inhabitants into slavery. They infiltrate the planet Zygerria disguised as slavers, and Anakin wins an audience with the planet's ruler, Queen Miraj. She invites him to a slave auction, where a terrible surprise awaits him.

## JEDI IN DISGUISE
On Zygerria, Anakin poses as slaver Lars Quell and claims to have eliminated one of Queen Miraj's enemies. Intrigued by the dashing stranger, Miraj accepts his gift: Ahsoka dressed as a slave girl!

# SLAVES OF THE REPUBLIC

"THOSE WHO ENSLAVE OTHERS INEVITABLY BECOME SLAVES THEMSELVES."

### NOTABLE CHARACTERS

Obi-Wan Kenobi

Anakin Skywalker

Queen Miraj

### VEHICLE

Zygerrian Slave Ship

### SLAVE FACILITY
The Zygerrian slave processing facility was originally designed to be used as one of the locations on Ryloth, seen in season 1.

### LOCATION

Zygerria

The Zygerrians' electro-whips shock their targets, stunning them into submission. It takes five whips to bring down Anakin.

**#78**
EPISODE 12, SEASON 4

**AIRDATE**
DECEMBER 2, 2011

**DIRECTOR**
BRIAN KALIN O'CONNELL

**WRITERS**
HENRY GILROY WIT
STEVEN MELCHING

**OBI-WAN FOR SALE**
Queen Miraj invites Anakin to a slave auction, where he discovers Obi-Wan has been captured and is for sale. Anakin risks everything to save his friend.

**GETTING CLOSE**
Anakin tries to free Obi-Wan, which intrigues Miraj. She seeks to win him to her side, knowing he will not harm her so long as Obi-Wan and Ahsoka are in her power.

**R2-D2 SALUTE**
Anakin's salute to R2-D2 in the slave market in this episode is reminiscent of the one Luke Skywalker gives R2 above the Sarlacc pit in Episode VI: *Return of the Jedi.*

**SPECIES**

**Brezak**

Anakin dons the clothes of a Zygerrian slaver with distaste, remembering his own childhood in Mos Espa, where he was a slave of Gardulla the Hutt and then Watto.

**"You are a man of many SURPRISES."**

QUEEN MIRAJ

**COUNT DOOKU** arrives on Zygerria to take Anakin captive and confront Queen Miraj about her growing alliance with the Jedi. Anakin escapes and rescues Ahsoka, but Dooku orders the execution of Obi-Wan and Captain Rex. They have been imprisoned in a slave facility along with the lost colonists from Kiros, on Queen Miraj's orders.

## OBI-WAN ENSLAVED
Obi-Wan has found the missing colonists of Kiros, but has been imprisoned with them on the planet Kadavo. He finds himself slipping into despair, worn down by the helpless life of a slave.

# ESCAPE FROM KADAVO

*"GREAT HOPE CAN COME FROM SMALL SACRIFICES."*

**NOTABLE CHARACTERS**

**Captain Rex**

**Keeper Agruss**

**Jedi Master Plo Koon**

Kadavo's slave processing facility is where evil Zygerrians dispose of rebellious or little-valued slaves.

**STARFIGHTERS**
The Zygerrian starfighters in this episode are based on concept art for the Imperial shuttle first seen in Episode VI: *Return of the Jedi*.

**#79**
EPISODE 13, SEASON 4

**AIRDATE**
JANUARY 6, 2012

**DIRECTOR**
DANNY KELLER

**WRITERS**
HENRY GILROY WIT
STEVEN MELCHING

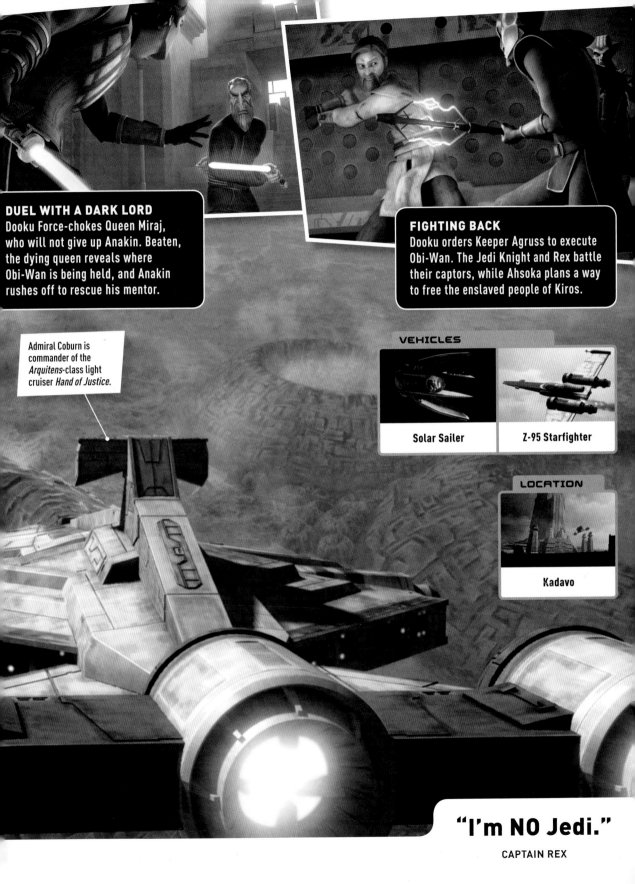

## DUEL WITH A DARK LORD
Dooku Force-chokes Queen Miraj, who will not give up Anakin. Beaten, the dying queen reveals where Obi-Wan is being held, and Anakin rushes off to rescue his mentor.

## FIGHTING BACK
Dooku orders Keeper Agruss to execute Obi-Wan. The Jedi Knight and Rex battle their captors, while Ahsoka plans a way to free the enslaved people of Kiros.

Admiral Coburn is commander of the *Arquitens*-class light cruiser *Hand of Justice*.

### VEHICLES

Solar Sailer

Z-95 Starfighter

### LOCATION

Kadavo

## "I'm NO Jedi."
CAPTAIN REX

**JUNIOR SENATOR** Lux Bonteri interrupts a peace conference on Mandalore to accuse Count Dooku of his mother's murder. Ahsoka saves Lux from execution for speaking against Dooku. Lux then takes her to Carlac, where she discovers that he has joined up with warriors of Death Watch, because they claim they will help him take revenge on Dooku.

## DANGEROUS ALLIES
Arriving on the snowy world of Carlac, Ahsoka is shocked to discover that Lux's allies in his fight against Dooku are the murderous commandos known as Death Watch.

### NOTABLE CHARACTERS

**Lux Bonteri**

**Ahsoka Tano**

**Governor Pre Vizsla**

### LOCATION

**Carlac**

Lux is devastated by the murder of his mother, Separatist Senator Mina Bonteri, killed by Dooku's thugs as she negotiated to end the Clone Wars.

**PRE VIZSLA'S LOOK**
The horned look of Pre Vizsla's new helmet was inspired by Doug Chiang's concept art for clone troopers for Episode II: *Attack of the Clones.*

# A FRIEND IN NEED

## "FRIENDSHIP SHOWS US WHO WE REALLY ARE."

| **#80** | **AIRDATE** | **DIRECTOR** | **WRITER** |
| --- | --- | --- | --- |
| EPISODE 14, SEASON 4 | JANUARY 13, 2013 | DAVE FILONI | CHRISTIAN TAYLOR |

## CRUEL PUNISHMENT

Lux soon learns the true nature of Death Watch. Their commander Pre Vizsla torches a Ming Po village on Carlac after they dare to rise up against him.

## CHALLENGING VIZSLA

Ahsoka tries to save the Ming Po, but is captured. R2-D2, who has been recruited by Death Watch to repair battle droids, cuts Ahsoka's bonds. She grabs her lightsaber and crosses blades with Vizsla.

### VEHICLES

*Phoenix*

**RGC-16 Airspeeder**

Vizsla had allied himself with Dooku, but broke from the Separatist leader when Dooku refused to back Death Watch's plan to invade Mandalore. The Count then scarred Vizsla's face with his lightsaber.

### OWL FACE

In this episode, Lux meets Bo-Katan, a Mandalorian warrior. Her helmet was inspired by a barn owl, as sketched by Dave Filoni. Her soldiers are called the Night Owls.

## "Welcome to DEATH Watch!"

PRE VIZSLA

# OBI-WAN IS APPARENTLY

killed by a sniper named Rako Hardeen. In fact, Kenobi's "death" is part of a Jedi plan for him to assume the identity of Hardeen and then unravel a conspiracy to assassinate Chancellor Palpatine. Will Obi-Wan succeed in infiltrating Moralo Eval and Cad Bane's criminal gang in prison? Can he foil their plan to kill the chancellor?

## PHYSICAL TRANSFORMATION
Obi-Wan has faked his own death. He then uses medical trickery to disguise himself as the bounty hunter Rako Hardeen. In his new form, he plans to take the place of Hardeen and infiltrate a Coruscant prison.

# DECEPTION

## "ALL WARFARE IS BASED ON DECEPTION."

### NOTABLE CHARACTERS

**Obi-Wan Kenobi (as Rako Hardeen)**

**Cad Bane**

**Moralo Eval**

**Yoda**

### IN MOURNING
At Obi-Wan's "funeral," Padmé, Senator Mon Mothma, and Duchess Satine wear black versions of their usual formal outfits.

**#81**
**EPISODE 15, SEASON 4**

**AIRDATE**
**JANUARY 20, 2012**

**DIRECTOR**
**KYLE DUNLEVY**

**WRITER**
**BRENT FRIEDMAN**

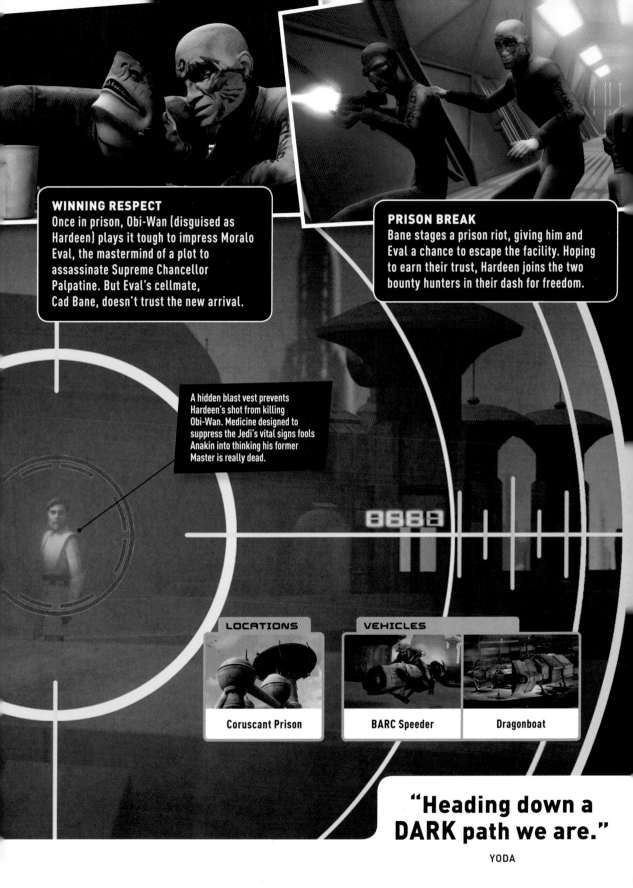

## WINNING RESPECT
Once in prison, Obi-Wan (disguised as Hardeen) plays it tough to impress Moralo Eval, the mastermind of a plot to assassinate Supreme Chancellor Palpatine. But Eval's cellmate, Cad Bane, doesn't trust the new arrival.

## PRISON BREAK
Bane stages a prison riot, giving him and Eval a chance to escape the facility. Hoping to earn their trust, Hardeen joins the two bounty hunters in their dash for freedom.

A hidden blast vest prevents Hardeen's shot from killing Obi-Wan. Medicine designed to suppress the Jedi's vital signs fools Anakin into thinking his former Master is really dead.

### LOCATIONS
**Coruscant Prison**

### VEHICLES
**BARC Speeder**

**Dragonboat**

"Heading down a DARK path we are."

YODA

**DISGUISED AS** bounty hunter Rako Hardeen, Obi-Wan flees Coruscant for Hutt Space with the criminals Moralo Eval and Cad Bane. He worms his way into Eval's trust to foil his plot to kill Palpatine. Rako must also win Bane's trust if he is to stay on track. Anakin, unaware that Obi-Wan is alive, is tracking the trio to take revenge on Hardeen for his Master's murder.

### TEST ON NAL HUTTA

Cad Bane distrusts Rako and tries to abandon him on the planet Nal Hutta, but Rako puts a homing beacon on Bane's ship and gives the frequency to the Hutts. They force down Bane and Eval, who find Rako waiting for them.

# FRIENDS AND ENEMIES

## "KEEP YOUR FRIENDS CLOSE, BUT KEEP YOUR ENEMIES CLOSER."

### NOTABLE CHARACTERS

**Anakin Skywalker**

**Obi-Wan Kenobi (as Rako Hardeen)**

**Moralo Eval**

Bane isn't a Neimoidian, but a member of the closely related Duros species, who generally dismiss their Neimoidian cousins as greedy and immature.

### INDIANA-STYLE

In this episode, Cad Bane briefly considers acquiring a fedora very much like the one worn by Indiana Jones.

### LOCATION

**Orondia**

| #82 EPISODE 16, SEASON 4 | AIRDATE JANUARY 27, 2012 | DIRECTOR BOSCO NG | WRITER BRENT FRIEDMAN |

## BEWARE THE DARK SIDE
Anakin pursues Obi-Wan's supposed killer, unaware of the plan he risks exposing. In frustration, he uses the Force to make a bartender on Nal Hutta reveal information about the bounty hunters' location.

## ANAKIN MAKES A MOVE
Anakin tracks the fugitives down and attacks Hardeen in a fury. Obi-Wan can neither let himself be defeated nor reveal himself. But what if one of them is hurt or killed?

**CODENAME**

Obi-Wan uses the codename "Ben" in his conversations with the Jedi Temple. He will return to that name during his exile on Tatooine.

Rako Hardeen got his facial tattoos while serving with the mercenary band known as Marvasa's Marauders in the Cyrillian Protectorate.

### VEHICLES

| YV-666 Light Freighter | Starhopper |
| --- | --- |

## "This is for OBI-WAN!"
ANAKIN SKYWALKER

**OBI-WAN**, working undercover
[as b]ounty hunter Rako Hardeen, arrives
[on S]erenno with Moralo Eval and Cad Bane,
[wher]e Count Dooku greets them. Obi-Wan and
[Bane] must compete alongside other notorious
[merc]enaries for places on Dooku's assassination
[team]. The competition takes place within The
[Box, ] a testing ground filled with deadly traps.

## GREEN GAS TEST
The 11 bounty hunters who enter The
Box immediately face peril: Deadly
dioxis gas seeps into the room. But
this is just the first challenge.

### CANTINA CONCEPT
Bounty hunter
Derrown is a Parwan,
a species whose design
dates back to unused
concept art for a cantina
patron in Episode IV,
*A New Hope*.

### SWAN HUNTER
The bounty hunter
Kiera Swan's name is an
homage to Elizabeth Swann,
Keira Knightley's character in
the *Pirates of the Caribbean*
movies. Knightley also played
Sabé in Episode I: *The
Phantom Menace*.

## NOTABLE CHARACTERS

**Obi-Wan Kenobi**

**Cad Bane**

**Count Dooku**

**Derrown**

**Embo**

**Moralo Eval**

**#83**
EPISODE 17, SEASON 4

**AIRDATE**
FEBRUARY 3, 2012

**DIRECTOR**
BRIAN KALIN
O'CONNELL

**WRITER**
BRENT FRIEDMAN

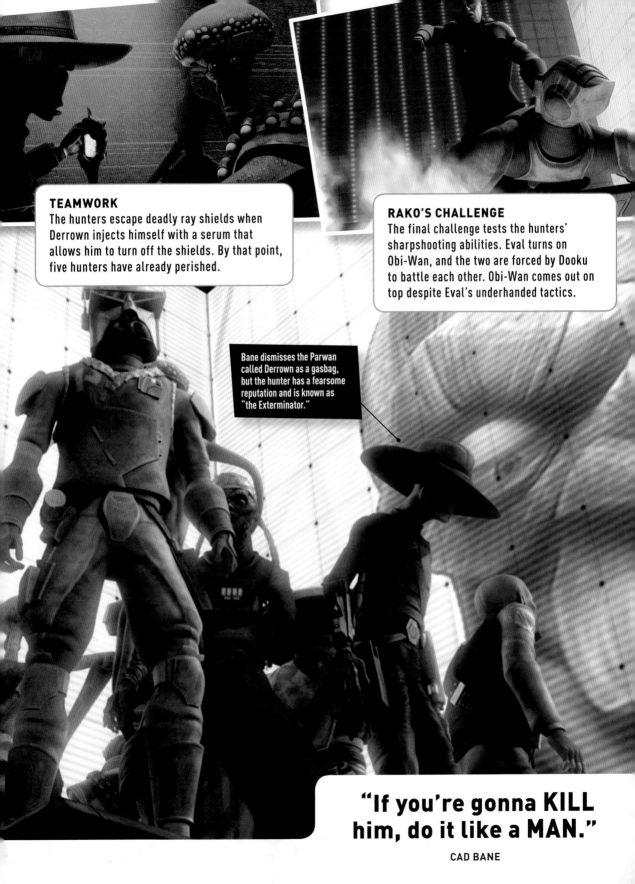

**TEAMWORK**
The hunters escape deadly ray shields when Derrown injects himself with a serum that allows him to turn off the shields. By that point, five hunters have already perished.

**RAKO'S CHALLENGE**
The final challenge tests the hunters' sharpshooting abilities. Eval turns on Obi-Wan, and the two are forced by Dooku to battle each other. Obi-Wan comes out on top despite Eval's underhanded tactics.

Bane dismisses the Parwan called Derrown as a gasbag, but the hunter has a fearsome reputation and is known as "the Exterminator."

**"If you're gonna KILL him, do it like a MAN."**
CAD BANE

**OBI WAN, DISGUISED** as the bounty hunter Rako Hardeen, has infiltrated Count Dooku's assassination plot against Chancellor Palpatine. The Jedi are protecting the Supreme Chancellor as he speaks at the Festival of Light on Naboo, but are unaware of Dooku's true plot against the Republic, and face more danger than they know.

## ATTACK ON THE CHANCELLOR
Obi-Wan, disguised as Rako, plans to shoot bounty hunter Derrown before he can destroy a shield generator protecting Palpatine. But Derrown succeeds in his task, throwing everything into chaos.

## BIBBLE'S DEBUT
The character Sio Bibble makes his *Clone Wars* debut in this episode. Bibble, played by Oliver Ford Davies, also appears in Episode I: *The Phantom Menace.*

If he captures Palpatine, Bane will have more credits than he can spend, and become the greatest bounty hunter in galactic history.

# CRISIS ON NABOO

### "TRUST IS THE GREATEST OF GIFTS, BUT IT MUST BE EARNED."

### VEHICLES

| | |
|---|---|
| **Luxury Yacht 3000** | **Flash Speeder** |

### NOTABLE CHARACTERS

| | | |
|---|---|---|
| **Obi-Wan Kenobi** | **Cad Bane** | **Chancellor Palpatine** |

**#84**
EPISODE 18, SEASON 4

**AIRDATE**
FEBRUARY 10, 2012

**DIRECTOR**
DANNY KELLER

**WRITER**
BRENT FRIEDMAN

**WHO'S WHO?**
The assassins use holographic matrixes to disguise their identities. This makes it hard to tell friend from foe—as Anakin discovers when Palpatine turns out to be Twazzi, another bounty hunter.

**THE DECEPTION ENDS**
Obi-Wan helps Palpatine escape and reveals his true identity to the bounty hunters. The Jedi take the hunters captive—the Jedi's elaborate plot has been successful. Yet the next morning, Obi-Wan is uneasy. He is right to be disturbed, Count Dooku is about to spring the real trap to capture Palpatine.

When Rako's true identity is revealed, Bane is angry but not particularly surprised. He knew trusting Hardeen was a mistake.

**LIGHT SHOW**
The fireworks display over Theed is a chronicle of Naboo's history—including scrolling yellow letters similar to the "crawl" that begins each *Star Wars* movie.

# "How MANY other LIES have I been told by the Council?"
ANAKIN SKYWALKER

**ASAJJ VENTRESS** returns to her homeworld Dathomir and becomes a full-fledged Nightsister, abandoning her Sith ambitions. Meanwhile, Count Dooku has not forgotten the Nightsisters' treachery and sends General Grievous to Dathomir to wipe out the witches. Asajj and the Nightsisters fight back by targeting Dooku with dark magic and summoning the dead.

## BLAZING SABERS
Grievous invades Dathomir with a massive army of droids and tanks. Standing against him is Ventress, who leads her sisters against her former allies, sabers blazing in the darkness.

## MASSACRE

"ONE MUST LET GO OF THE PAST TO HOLD ON TO THE FUTURE."

### NOTABLE CHARACTERS

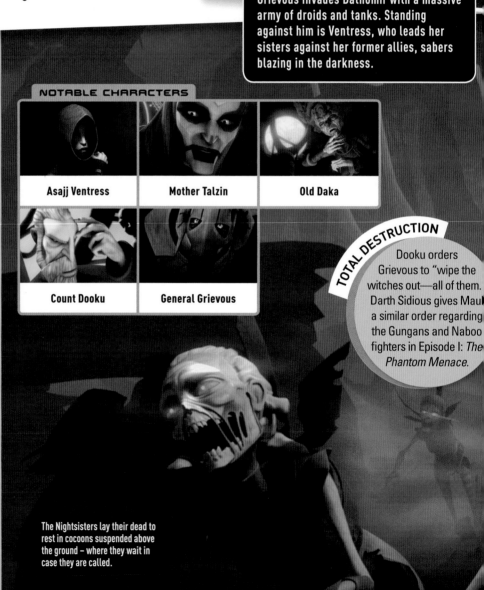

| | | |
|---|---|---|
| Asajj Ventress | Mother Talzin | Old Daka |
| Count Dooku | General Grievous | |

### TOTAL DESTRUCTION
Dooku orders Grievous to "wipe the witches out—all of them." Darth Sidious gives Maul a similar order regarding the Gungans and Naboo fighters in Episode I: *The Phantom Menace.*

The Nightsisters lay their dead to rest in cocoons suspended above the ground – where they wait in case they are called.

| #85 EPISODE 19, SEASON 4 | AIRDATE FEBRUARY 24, 2012 | DIRECTOR STEWARD LEE | WRITER KATIE LUCAS |
|---|---|---|---|

**DARK MAGIC**
Mother Talzin strikes back at Dooku, using a charm that inflicts excruciating pain on the Count. Dooku tries frantically to contact Grievous, commanding him to break the deadly spell.

**GRIEVOUS VS. ASAJJ**
Grievous battles Ventress, who challenges him to prove he's the greater warrior. But the cyborg warlord is not interested in bragging rights—and tells his droids to open fire on Ventress.

An eldritch green glow is a telltale sign of Nightsister magic at work.

**WITCHES' GRAVES**
The Nightsisters' animal-skin graves in this episode are housed in treelike structures made of branches, bones, and shells.

**"Prepare yourselves, sisters—the WAR has COME to Dathomir."**

MOTHER TALZIN

**FORCED INTO EXILE** after her clan, the Nightsisters, are destroyed, Asajj Ventress joins a team of bounty hunters led by Boba Fett. On a mission to Quarzite, they race through the planet's eerie caverns aboard a subtram, defending a mysterious chest against shadowy attackers. Will Ventress hold her own among the bounty hunters?

**A SURPRISE ATTACK**
Ventress joins Fett's mercenaries in protecting a chest on its way to Otua Blank, Quarzite's ruler. But mysterious Kage attackers emerge from the darkness to attack the hunters.

## BOUNTY

"WHO WE ARE NEVER CHANGES: WHO WE THINK WE ARE DOES."

**NOTABLE CHARACTERS**

**Asajj Ventress**

**Boba Fett**

**Krismo Sodi**

**Pluma Sodi**

The caverns of Quarzite are home to the mysterious Kage, who have rebelled against the brutal rule of the Belugan warlord Otua Blank and stage raids from the backs of their multi-legged milodons.

**KRISMO CONCEPT**
Krismo's character design was inspired by Iain McCaig's concept art for Obi-Wan Kenobi in Episode I: *The Phantom Menace.*

**VEHICLES**

**Hound's Tooth**

**Subtram**

**#86**
EPISODE 20, SEASON 4

**AIRDATE**
MARCH 2, 2012

**DIRECTOR**
KYLE DUNLEVY

**WRITER**
KATIE LUCAS

## DESPERATE DEFENSE
As the warriors continue to attack, Fett's hunters close ranks to defend the chest. They don't know what's inside—only that the warriors are willing to die to get it.

## CHOOSING SIDES
Boba knocks over the chest—and out rolls a young Kage girl named Pluma who has been kidnapped against her will to be Otua's bride. The lead Kage warrior is her brother, Krismo, and he is determined to rescue her. All appears to be lost for Krismo and Pluma until an unlikely ally comes to their aid.

The Kage are superb fighters whether armed with their electro-swords or merely their hands and feet.

SPECIES

Milodon

LOCATION

Quarzite

## "I want what's MINE!"
KRISMO SODI

**BOTH JEDI AND SITH** sense dark stirrings in the Force. Ripples in its energy are being created by Savage Opress's quest to find his lost brother—who is none other than the Sith warrior Darth Maul. Savage's search takes him to the forsaken junkyard world of Lotho Minor. When he falls far into the planet's depths, he makes a stunning discovery.

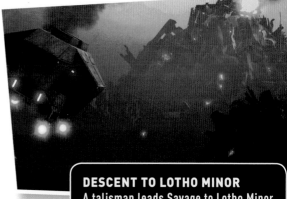

### DESCENT TO LOTHO MINOR
A talisman leads Savage to Lotho Minor. Buried deep in junk and scoured by acid rain, it is a perfect hideaway for the forgotten and the insane.

Junkers are wandering scavengers clad in metal and are apparently part machine. The origin of these bizarre nomads is one of the galaxy's many mysteries.

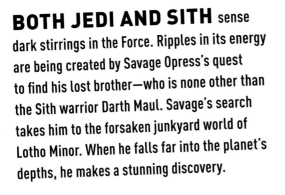

## BROTHERS

*"A FALLEN ENEMY MAY RISE AGAIN, BUT THE RECONCILED ONE IS TRULY VANQUISHED."*

### LOCATIONS

**Stobar**

**Lotho Minor**

### DROIDS

**Waitress Droid**

**Fire-Breather**

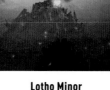

### NOTABLE CHARACTERS

**Darth Maul**

**Savage Opress**

**Morley**

**MAUL'S TRADEMARK**

The introductory *Star Wars* logo in the opening credits of this episode is in Darth Maul's iconic red, not the usual yellow.

**#87**
EPISODE 21, SEASON 4

**AIRDATE**
MARCH 9, 2012

**DIRECTOR**
BOSCO NG

**WRITER**
KATIE LUCAS

**TALES FROM THE DEEP**
Savage acquires a guide: a slippery, treacherous Anacondan named Morley. Savage tells Morley tales of a horned man rumored to dwell somewhere below the surface of the planet.

**MAUL REVEALED**
In the planet's depths, Savage confronts a shambling figure, its lower body and mind gone. This frightening yet pathetic creature is what remains of his brother Darth Maul.

Savage has grown more powerful since escaping from Dooku and Ventress. He has used his anger and pain to open him more fully to dark side energies.

**SERPENT GUIDE**
The snakelike Morley is a member of the Anacondan species. Another Anacondan works as a bartender on Coruscant in the episode "Deception."

**"Something is RISING... something SINISTER."**

COUNT DOOKU

## SAVAGE OPRESS BRINGS

the damaged Darth Maul to Dathomir, where Nightsister Mother Talzin cures his madness and gives him new cybernetic legs. Obsessed by his hunger for revenge, Maul slaughters the colonists of the planet Raydonia and challenges Obi-Wan to confront him. When Obi-Wan arrives on Raydonia, a dark and terrifying showdown looms between Jedi and Sith.

**UNDER A SPELL**
On Dathomir, Mother Talzin uses her spells to close the cracks in Maul's mind, drawing forth the madness of his long and lonely exile, and restoring his sanity.

## REVENGE

### "THE ENEMY OF MY ENEMY IS MY FRIEND."

### NOTABLE CHARACTERS

**Darth Maul**

**Obi-Wan Kenobi**

**Asajj Ventress**

### LOCATION

**Raydonia**

### VEHICLE

**Turtle Tanker**

**A FAMILIAR PLACE**

In this episode, Asajj Ventress is seen in the Mos Eisley cantina from Episode IV: *A New Hope*. The bar is also seen in the episodes "Sphere of Influence" and "Bounty."

**#88**
EPISODE 22, SEASON 4

**AIRDATE**
MARCH 16, 2012

**DIRECTOR**
BRIAN KALIN O'CONNELL

**WRITER**
KATIE LUCAS

**SEEKING REVENGE**

Tottering uncertainly on his new cybernetic legs, Maul still seems lost. But when Savage hands him a lightsaber, his uncertainty is replaced by resolve. He will have revenge.

**STRANGE ALLY**

Obi-Wan is captured by Maul and Savage, but is then rescued by the last person he expected: Asajj Ventress. Together, the unlikely allies fight the Sith brothers.

**CYBORG FORM**

ILM art director Aaron McBride designed Maul's cyborg form for the 2005 graphic novel *Star Wars: Visionaries* (2005), in which Maul returns to Tatooine in search of Kenobi.

**"I have been WAITING for you."**

DARTH MAUL

## WITH THE REPUBLIC

bogged down fighting the Separatists, Anakin suggests training rebels to lead insurgencies on a number of worlds. To test the idea, he travels with Obi-Wan and Ahsoka to Onderon, where rebels are fighting a Separatist-aligned king. The three Jedi work to teach the techniques of war—and the art of leadership.

## TEACHING TECHNIQUES

As veterans of many battles against Separatist droids, the Jedi and Captain Rex prove ideal teachers for instructing Onderon's rebels in effective techniques for combating everything from AATs to droidekas.

Lux Bonteri grew up on Onderon, and briefly represented it in the Separatist Senate. He has now returned to battle the Separatists.

# A WAR ON TWO FRONTS

"FEAR IS A MALLEABLE WEAPON."

### RUPINGS

The four-eyed avians used as mounts by the Onderon rebels are known as "rupings" in honor of concept artist Tara Rueping.

### NOTABLE CHARACTERS

| Steela Gerrera | Saw Gerrera | Lux Bonteri |
| --- | --- | --- |

**#89**
EPISODE 2, SEASON 5

**AIRDATE**
OCTOBER 6, 2012

**DIRECTOR**
DAVE FILONI

**WRITER**
CHRIS COLLINS

## TROUBLE ON THE WAY
Squads of battle droids march from the Separatist-held capital city of Iziz to destroy the rebel camp. Insurgent leaders Saw and Steela must show that they have learned their lessons.

## REBEL DISGUISE
After defeating the droids sent to destroy them, the rebels begin the next stage of their campaign: infiltrating Iziz disguised as a caravan of jungle hunters. The battle has only just begun....

Steela is an expert sharpshooter whose cool under fire commands increasing respect among the Onderon rebels.

### ANAKIN IMPRESSED
Anakin calls Steela's ability with a rifle "impressive, most impressive," a line he will repeat as Darth Vader in Episode V: *Empire Strikes Back.*

Steela's brother, Saw, is a brave fighter and charismatic leader, but limited by his impetuousness and hot temper.

SPECIES

**Falumpaset**

DROID

**Battle Droid Commander**

## "We can only PROTECT them—we cannot fight this WAR for them."
OBI-WAN KENOBI

WITH AHSOKA'S assistance, Onderon's rebels bring their campaign to the capital, Iziz, destroying Separatist units and working to rally the people to their cause. Amid rising tensions between Saw Gerrera and Steela Gerrera over who will lead the group, the rebels decide to strike the city's main power generator, so the battle droids will be unable to recharge.

## TWO KINGS
With attacks spreading, King Rash of Onderon orders Dendup, his imprisoned predecessor, to stop the insurgency. The former king says he can do nothing: The rebel movement comes from the people.

# FRONT-RUNNERS
## "TO SEEK SOMETHING IS TO BELIEVE IN ITS POSSIBILITY."

A super battle droid's diagnostic readout sits right above its maintenance access port. The port is a vulnerable spot, but a difficult target to hit.

### WILD FOUNTAIN
The fountain in the plaza in Iziz shows an Onderonian riding a rearing dalgo, with falumpasets spewing water from their mouths.

**#90**
EPISODE 3, SEASON 5

**AIRDATE**
OCTOBER 13, 2012

**DIRECTOR**
STEWARD LEE

**WRITER**
CHRIS COLLINS

188

## A PLAN

Lux Bonteri argues that the rebels can win over the people by hitting a big, symbolic target. They decide to demonstrate their strength by targeting the city's main power generator.

## STEELA ON TANK

The rebels lure a droid patrol by calling for backup, then capture the tank. But the main power generator is heavily guarded. This won't be easy....

### IZIZ SPEEDERS

The landspeeders seen in Iziz are the same model as those driven by Bail Organa in Episode III: *Revenge of the Sith*.

Super battle droids can use firearms, but most rely on their powerful built-in blaster cannons.

### NOTABLE CHARACTERS

| | |
|---|---|
| Ahsoka Tano | Lux Bonteri |
| King Rash | King Dendup |
| Saw Gerrera | Steela Gerrera |

"The people need to BELIEVE we can SUCCEED."

STEELA GERRERA

NOW THAT SHE IS leader of the Onderon rebels, Steela Gerrera orders her group to step up their strikes against King Rash's forces. She also appeals to the people via hidden holoprojectors to overthrow Rash. When the former king, Dendup, says he can't stop the insurgency, a furious Rash orders his execution. Steela's brother, Saw Gerrera, decides on a risky plan to save the former king.

## TRAPPED

Saw breaks into the royal palace in an ill-advised attempt to rescue Dendup—one that ends with him trapped and captured by King Rash.

# THE SOFT WAR

### "STRUGGLES OFTEN BEGIN AND END WITH THE TRUTH."

### DROID

**Super Tactical Droid**

### LOCATION

**Onderon**

### NOTABLE CHARACTERS

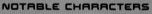

**Saw Gerrera**

**General Tandin**

**King Dendup**

|  | **#91**<br>EPISODE 4, SEASON 5 | **AIRDATE**<br>OCTOBER 20, 2012 | **DIRECTOR**<br>KYLE DUNLEVY | **WRITER**<br>CHRIS COLLINS |

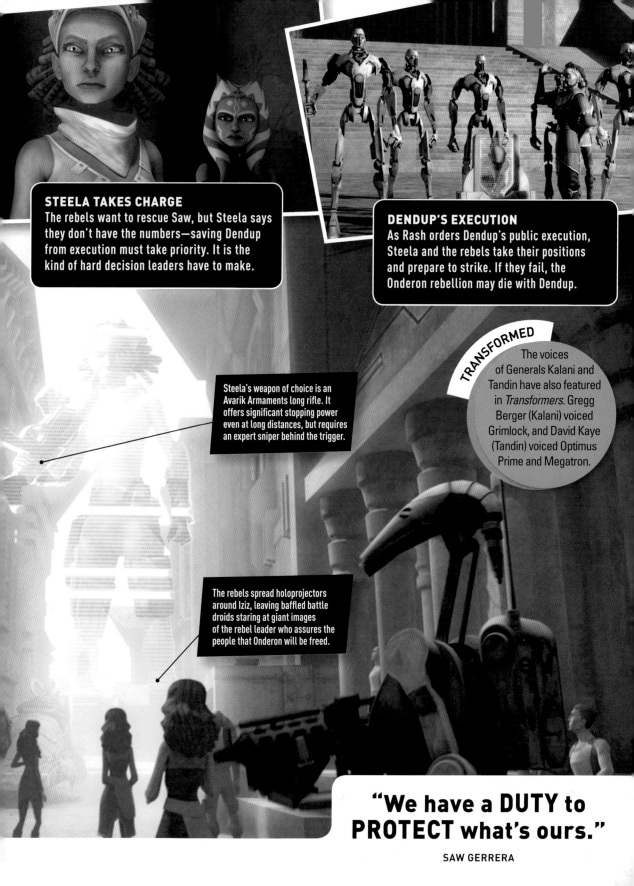

## STEELA TAKES CHARGE
The rebels want to rescue Saw, but Steela says they don't have the numbers—saving Dendup from execution must take priority. It is the kind of hard decision leaders have to make.

## DENDUP'S EXECUTION
As Rash orders Dendup's public execution, Steela and the rebels take their positions and prepare to strike. If they fail, the Onderon rebellion may die with Dendup.

### TRANSFORMED
The voices of Generals Kalani and Tandin have also featured in *Transformers*. Gregg Berger (Kalani) voiced Grimlock, and David Kaye (Tandin) voiced Optimus Prime and Megatron.

Steela's weapon of choice is an Avarik Armaments long rifle. It offers significant stopping power even at long distances, but requires an expert sniper behind the trigger.

The rebels spread holoprojectors around Iziz, leaving baffled battle droids staring at giant images of the rebel leader who assures the people that Onderon will be freed.

## "We have a DUTY to PROTECT what's ours."
SAW GERRERA

**THE PEOPLE OF IZIZ** rise up against their Separatist captors, prompting King Rash to send droid gunships to destroy the rebels' base of operations. The rebels are no match for the gunships, and Ahsoka begs Anakin and Obi-Wan for help. The Republic cannot intervene in what it sees as an internal conflict, but Anakin has an idea that might save Onderon's freedom fighters.

## REBEL SUPPORT

Onderon's former king, Dendup, has been freed from King Rash's forces. The rebels have his support, as well as that of Onderon's people and General Tandin.

# TIPPING POINTS

## "DISOBEDIENCE IS A DEMAND FOR CHANGE."

The droid gunships' photoreceptors and pronounced prow look like a face, giving the mechanical aircraft the appearance of an avian predator.

The gunships' turrets rotate and seek targets independently, allowing a single gunship to attack many targets on the ground or in the air.

### NOTABLE CHARACTERS

**Steela Gerrera**

**Hondo Ohnaka**

**King Dendup**

### VEHICLE

**Droid Gunship**

| #92 EPISODE 5, SEASON 5 | AIRDATE OCTOBER 27, 2012 | DIRECTOR BOSCO NG | WRITER CHRIS COLLINS |

## MISSILES TO THE RESCUE
The Separatists strike back with gunships, hoping to destroy King Dendup. It looks like Steela's rebels will be crushed, but Anakin convinces pirate Hondo Ohnaka to bring them a cache of powerful missiles.

## STEELA IN PERIL
Steela saves Dendup from the Separatist assault, but a near-miss by a gunship leaves her clinging to the edge of a cliff. Despite Lux and Ahsoka's best efforts, she does not survive.

### SOUND EFFECTS
The distinctive engine sound of the droid gunships was created by filtering and mixing together recordings of a buzzsaw, a truck's diesel engine, and a human scream.

### SPECIES

| Dalgo | Fambaa | Ruping |
| --- | --- | --- |

### PARALLEL TALK
After Ahsoka praises Steela's courage, Lux asks, "What good would that do if she gets herself killed?" Princess Leia and Luke Skywalker have a similar conversation about Han Solo in Episode IV: A New Hope.

## "We all want VICTORY— but not at the cost of INNOCENT lives."
STEELA GERRERA

**AHSOKA LEADS SIX** younglings to the icy world of Ilum for the Gathering: An important ritual during which promising Jedi learn from Yoda and undergo trials to find living crystals that will power their lightsabers. The greatest tests faced by these future Jedi come not from the frozen conditions on Ilum, but from their own doubts and weaknesses, which they must overcome.

## FACING THEIR FEARS

To find their crystals, the younglings must confront their own weaknesses. For example, the Ithorian youngling Byph must face his fear of the unknown.

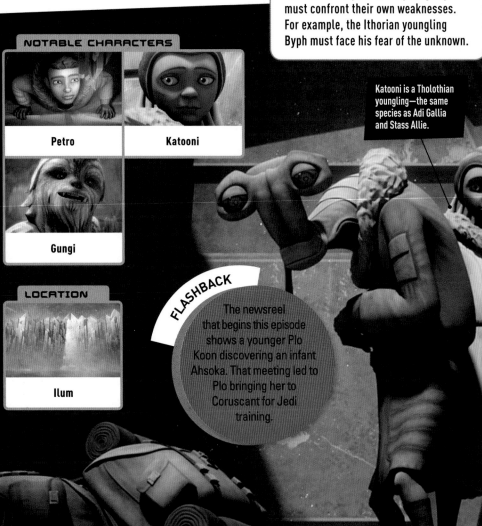

Katooni is a Tholothian youngling—the same species as Adi Gallia and Stass Allie.

### NOTABLE CHARACTERS

**Petro**

**Katooni**

**Gungi**

### LOCATION

**Ilum**

**FLASHBACK**

The newsreel that begins this episode shows a younger Plo Koon discovering an infant Ahsoka. That meeting led to Plo bringing her to Coruscant for Jedi training.

# THE GATHERING

"HE WHO FACES HIMSELF, FINDS HIMSELF."

**#93**
EPISODE 6, SEASON 5

**AIRDATE**
NOVEMBER 3, 2012

**DIRECTOR**
KYLE DUNLEVY

**WRITER**
CHRISTIAN TAYLO

**A LESSON LEARNED**
Gungi, the Wookiee youngling, cannot cross the thin ice atop a subterranean lake. His answer is patience—if he waits, shadows will cover the lake and the ice will thicken.

**PETRO TRIUMPHANT**
If they can overcome the obstacles that face them, the younglings will emerge with their own crystals. That's reason for celebration, as Corellian youngling Petro discovers.

**COAT COLOR**
Zatt's coat is a smaller version of Han's in Episode V: *The Empire Strikes Back.* To add fuel to debates about whether Han's coat was blue or brown—note that Zatt's is blue.

Rodian youngling Ganodi has a bad habit of letting her frustrations interfere with her connection to the Force.

**"If JEDI you are to BECOME, enter the CRYSTAL cave you must."**

YODA

## ABOARD THE STAR CRUISER

*Crucible*, Jedi younglings meet a new teacher: An ancient droid named Professor Huyang, who instructs them in how to build their lightsabers. Their lessons are interrupted by a pirate attack—Hondo Ohnaka wants the valuable Kyber crystals they are using to make their lightsabers. When the marauders invade their ship, Ahsoka and the younglings must outwit them.

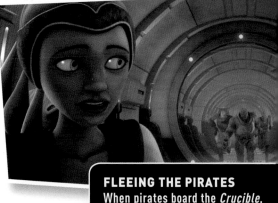

### FLEEING THE PIRATES
When pirates board the *Crucible*, Ahsoka orders the Padawans to hide in the ventilation system. But Hondo's pirates smoke them out with gas grenades.

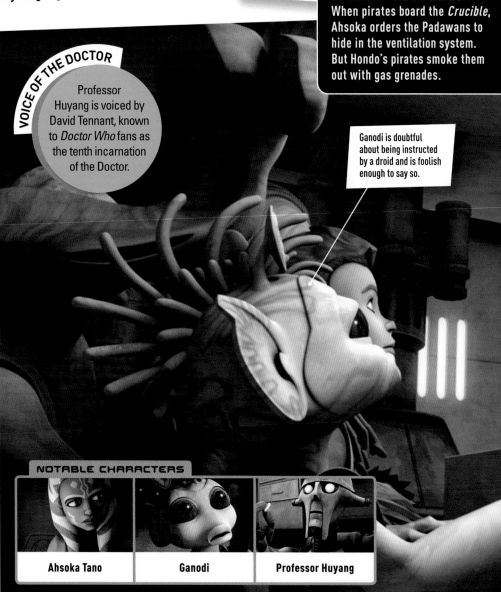

## A TEST OF STRENGTH

### "THE YOUNG ARE OFTEN UNDERESTIMATED."

**VOICE OF THE DOCTOR**

Professor Huyang is voiced by David Tennant, known to *Doctor Who* fans as the tenth incarnation of the Doctor.

Ganodi is doubtful about being instructed by a droid and is foolish enough to say so.

### NOTABLE CHARACTERS

| Ahsoka Tano | Ganodi | Professor Huyang |
| --- | --- | --- |

**#94**
EPISODE 7, SEASON 5

**AIRDATE**
NOVEMBER 10, 2012

**DIRECTOR**
BOSCO NG

**WRITER**
CHRISTIAN TAYLOR

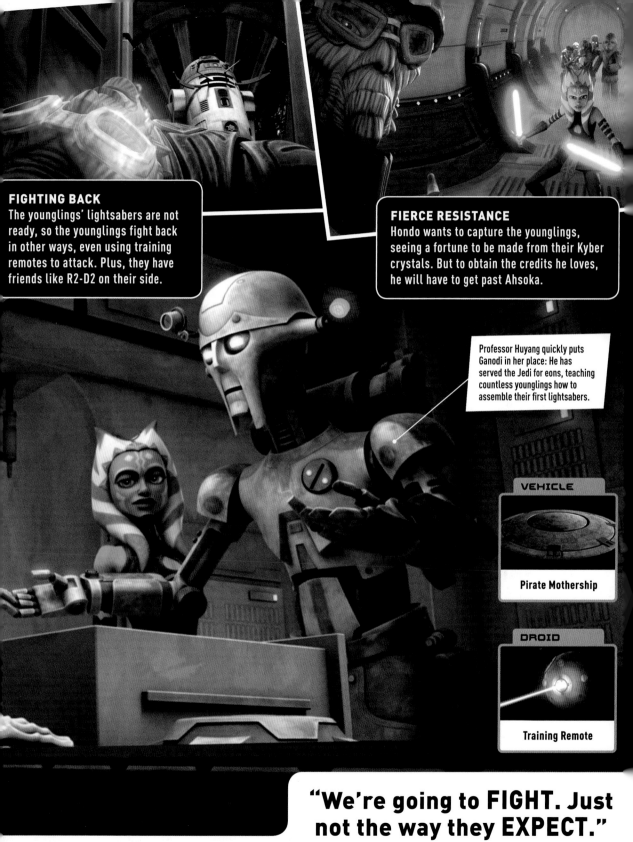

## FIGHTING BACK

The younglings' lightsabers are not ready, so the younglings fight back in other ways, even using training remotes to attack. Plus, they have friends like R2-D2 on their side.

## FIERCE RESISTANCE

Hondo wants to capture the younglings, seeing a fortune to be made from their Kyber crystals. But to obtain the credits he loves, he will have to get past Ahsoka.

Professor Huyang quickly puts Ganodi in her place: He has served the Jedi for eons, teaching countless younglings how to assemble their first lightsabers.

**VEHICLE**

**Pirate Mothership**

**DROID**

**Training Remote**

## "We're going to FIGHT. Just not the way they EXPECT."

AHSOKA TANO

# BOUND FOR RESCUE

## "WHEN WE RESCUE OTHERS, WE RESCUE OURSELVES."

**AHSOKA HAS BEEN** captured by Hondo Ohnaka's pirates, but Obi-Wan orders the younglings aboard the Crucible to wait for help instead of attempting a rescue. After building their lightsabers, the younglings ignore Obi-Wan and decide to save Ahsoka. When they encounter the circus known as Preigo's Traveling World of Wonder, they see an opportunity to go undercover.

### OBI-WAN UNDER ATTACK
Obi-Wan intends to send Commander Cody and his troops to rescue Ahsoka. His plans are hindered when Grievous launches a surprise attack on them.

### NOTABLE CHARACTERS

**Zatt**

**Byph**

**Preigo**

**SWEET MUSIC**

The Gamorrean in clown makeup plays the same model organ used by Max Rebo in Episode VI: *Return of the Jedi*.

Preigo's waxed mustache is the envy of every Dug this side of Malastare.

**#95**
EPISODE 8, SEASON 5

**AIRDATE**
NOVEMBER 17, 2012

**DIRECTOR**
BRIAN KALIN O'CONNELL

**WRITER**
CHRISTIAN TAYLOR

### YOUNGLINGS IN DISGUISE
On Florrum, the younglings encounter Preigo and his traveling carnival. Calling on their Force skills, the younglings claim they are a troupe of acrobats: the Animal Instincts!

### TAKING A GAMBLE
The Animal Instincts invite Hondo to join them for their show's final stunt. It is a trick that could end with Ahsoka rescued—or all of them imprisoned by the pirates.

### FEARSOME FASHION
Several of the younglings disguise themselves as *Star Wars* beasties. Zatt is a rancor and Petro is a gundark, while Gungi is a narglatch.

Hondo stole his prized overcoat from a Wroonian noble, who was captured for ransom by his pirates.

### VEHICLES

*Crucible*

**Preigo's Traveling World of Wonder**

## "Don't WORRY, we have a PLAN ... I think."
KATOONI

**AHSOKA AND** the younglings flee Hondo Ohnaka's pirates in a stolen speeder, but are quickly recaptured by Ohnaka's accomplices. Returning to their base on Florrum with their captives, the pirates discover that General Grievous has invaded and taken over their base, seizing Hondo. Needing a way off Florrum, the Jedi agree to help their pirate captors to rescue Hondo from the Separatists.

### REVENGE OF GRIEVOUS
General Grievous's master, Count Dooku, has not forgotten that Hondo once held him for ransom. Now, the pirate pays the price for his disrespect: Hondo will serve the Separatist cause or die.

# A NECESSARY BOND

## "CHOOSE YOUR ENEMIES WISELY, AS THEY MAY BE YOUR LAST HOPE."

Gwarm is a longtime lieutenant of Hondo's, having fought beside the pirate boss on many raids and missions.

**VEHICLE**

**Combat Speeder**

**NOTABLE CHARACTERS**

| | | |
|---|---|---|
| Ganodi | General Grievous | Hondo Ohnaka |

**200**

**#96**
EPISODE 9, SEASON 5

**AIRDATE**
NOVEMBER 24, 2012

**DIRECTOR**
DANNY KELLER

**WRITER**
CHRISTIAN TAYLOR

## JEDI AND PIRATES TOGETHER
Ahsoka and Gwarm lead a band of pirates and younglings into the occupied base. They free Hondo and wade into the ranks of battle droids, swinging lightsabers and vibroswords.

## AHSOKA VS. GRIEVOUS
A Jedi youngling named Katooni escapes with Hondo and his pirates in *Slave I*, but Grievous catches up with the other younglings. Only Ahsoka can stop him from adding more lightsabers to his collection.

Although Professor Huyang's arms have been severed by the pirates, his cognitive unit remains intact.

### ART OF HUYANG
Huyang's design draws inspiration from concept art of C-3PO and other early sketches by legendary illustrator Ralph McQuarrie.

## "So many LIGHTSABERS to ADD to my collection!"
GENERAL GRIEVOUS

THE JEDI HAVE intercepted a secret transmission from General Grievous, but they cannot understand it without an encryption code, which is well-guarded aboard a Separatist ship. In order to steal the code, the Jedi prepare an unlikely strike team: four astromechs and a modified pit droid. Known as D-Squad, these droids are led by the diminutive Colonel Gascon.

**D-SQUAD ATTACK**
After boarding the Separatist warship, the droids of D-Squad take more direct action than Gascon had in mind, attacking the battle droids escorting them for interrogation.

Colonel Gascon is tough and no-nonsense, even at only 33 centimeters tall. But the little officer has a big secret: His combat experience is limited to reading maps.

# SECRET WEAPONS

## "HUMILITY IS THE ONLY DEFENSE AGAINST HUMILIATION."

**#97**
EPISODE 10, SEASON 5

**AIRDATE**
DECEMBER 1, 2012

**DIRECTOR**
DANNY KELLER

**WRITER**
BRENT FRIEDMAN

202

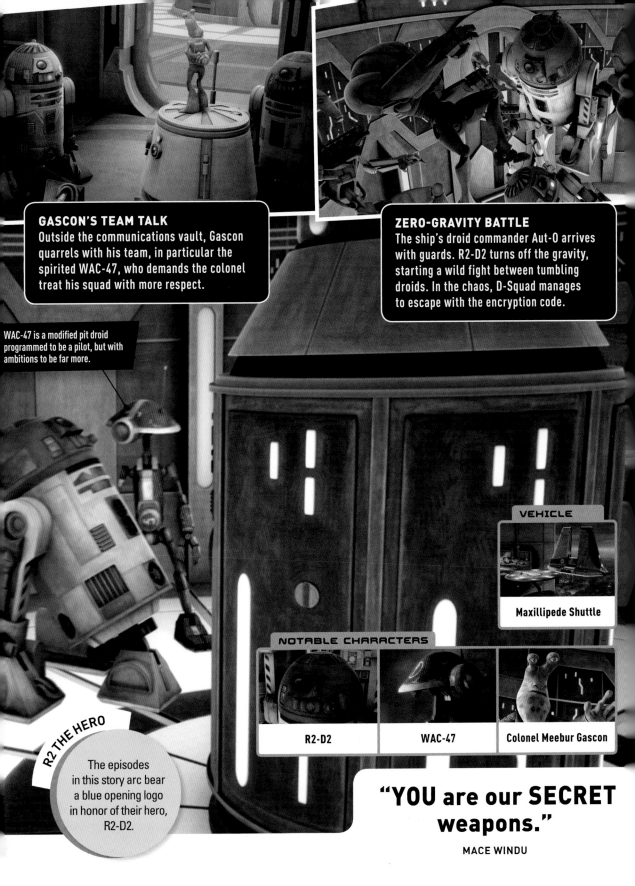

## GASCON'S TEAM TALK
Outside the communications vault, Gascon quarrels with his team, in particular the spirited WAC-47, who demands the colonel treat his squad with more respect.

WAC-47 is a modified pit droid programmed to be a pilot, but with ambitions to be far more.

## ZERO-GRAVITY BATTLE
The ship's droid commander Aut-O arrives with guards. R2-D2 turns off the gravity, starting a wild fight between tumbling droids. In the chaos, D-Squad manages to escape with the encryption code.

**VEHICLE**

Maxillipede Shuttle

**NOTABLE CHARACTERS**

| R2-D2 | WAC-47 | Colonel Meebur Gascon |
| --- | --- | --- |

**R2 THE HERO**

The episodes in this story arc bear a blue opening logo in honor of their hero, R2-D2.

## "YOU are our SECRET weapons."

MACE WINDU

## THE REPUBLIC'S D-Squad

of droids is on its way back to Coruscant when a comet swarm causes them to crash on the forsaken planet Abafar. To survive, they must cross a featureless desert known as the Void, which is without landmarks, water, or power. While the droids make progress, the wilderness threatens Colonel Gascon's sanity.

### R2 TAKES CONTROL

R2-D2 leads D-Squad in a straight line away from the crash site. It is as good a plan as any if they are to get back to Coruscant and deliver their crucial encryption code to the Jedi.

### RABBIT SUIT

The skeleton found in the shuttle wears a suit similar to that of Jaxxon, a man-sized green rabbit introduced in Marvel Comics' *Star Wars* comics in 1978. The skull even has long incisors.

# A SUNNY DAY IN THE VOID

"WHEN ALL SEEMS HOPELESS, A TRUE HERO GIVES HOPE."

**#98**
EPISODE 11, SEASON 5

**AIRDATE**
DECEMBER 8, 2012

**DIRECTOR**
KYLE DUNLEVY

**WRITER**
BRENT FRIEDMAN

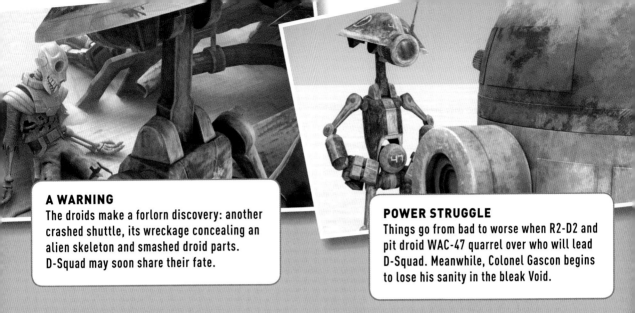

### A WARNING
The droids make a forlorn discovery: another crashed shuttle, its wreckage concealing an alien skeleton and smashed droid parts. D-Squad may soon share their fate.

### POWER STRUGGLE
Things go from bad to worse when R2-D2 and pit droid WAC-47 quarrel over who will lead D-Squad. Meanwhile, Colonel Gascon begins to lose his sanity in the bleak Void.

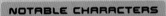

### NOTABLE CHARACTERS

**Colonel Meebur Gascon**

**QT-KT**

**M5-BZ**

### SPECIES

**Void Strider**

Abafar's curious atmosphere conceals its sun, rendering the entire sky a painfully bright orange and further disorientating those condemned to wander the Void.

Abafar's surface is featureless white hardpan, so travelers leave no tracks as evidence of where they have been.

### COMIC INSPIRATION
This episode began with George Lucas's desire to create "an episode about nothing," recalling the work of legendary French comic book artist Moebius.

## "Look on the BRIGHT SIDE, Colonel—at least it is a sunny day."

**STILL STRANDED** on Abafar, Colonel Gascon and D-Squad visit the run-down town of Pons Ora and meet clone commando Gregor, who has lost his memory and is now a dishwasher in a filthy diner. Gascon hopes to unlock Gregor's mind so the clone will help them escape the Separatist-controlled planet and reach an orbiting Jedi cruiser.

**A LOST CLONE**
Bigoted chef Borkus refuses to serve Gascon a meal in his diner, forcing the hungry colonel to scrounge in the garbage. There, Gascon is stunned to find a clone dressed in civilian clothes.

Clone commandos such as Gregor are engineered for more independent thought than standard troopers, and are given extensive training in covert missions ranging from infiltration to sabotage.

**SULLUSTANS**
Borkus is a Sullustan, a species first seen in Episode VI: *Return of the Jedi*. Borkus is the first Sullustan to appear in the television series.

| #99 EPISODE 12, SERIES 5 | AIRDATE JANUARY 5, 2013 | DIRECTOR STEWARD LEE | WRITER BRENT FRIEDMAN |

## DROIDS TO THE RESCUE
D-Squad and Gascon help Gregor remember who he is. But before they can escape Abafar, D-Squad must confront Borkus, who is furious at the prospect of losing his slave.

## GREGOR HELPS D-SQUAD
Remembering his training, Gregor battles a squad of Separatist droids while D-Squad races for the shuttle. The clone commando prepares to sacrifice himself to save D-Squad.

The DC-17m is the weapon of choice for clone commandos, as it can be reconfigured for a variety of combat jobs.

### DROID

**CLL-M2 Ordnance Lifter**

### NOTABLE CHARACTERS

**Clone Commando Gregor**

**Borkus**

**Colonel Meebur Gascon**

### FUNNY SIGNS
Sharp-eyed viewers will spot a number of in-jokes if they can read Aurebesh signs, such as the Abafar Junior Dejarik Club, which doesn't allow Wookiees.

## "SIMPLE isn't good enough anymore. Not for THIS clone."
GREGOR

**D-SQUAD ESCAPES** Separatists on Abafar and boards an orbiting Jedi Cruiser. The ship is on course for the space station *Valor*, where a Republic strategy conference is being held, but all is not as it should be. Can R2-D2 and the rest of Colonel Gascon's D-Squad of droids overpower Separatist saboteurs and prevent an attack that could change the outcome of the war?

## A SEPARATIST PLOT
On the Jedi Cruiser's bridge, D-Squad makes a disturbing discovery: The clone officers are holograms, and Separatist droids have taken over the ship!

Ships traveling through hyperspace move at such high speeds that passing stars become a blur of light.

# POINT OF NO RETURN

"YOU MUST TRUST IN OTHERS OR SUCCESS IS IMPOSSIBLE."

### NOTABLE CHARACTERS

**R2-D2**

**Colonel Meebur Gascon**

**WAC-47**

### EVOLUTION OF GASCON
Colonel Gascon resembles Episode I concept art for Gungans. In fact, Gascon is a Zilkin: a similar-looking, intelligent species.

### LOCATION

**Space Station *Valor***

| #100 | AIRDATE | DIRECTOR | WRITER |
|---|---|---|---|
| EPISODE 13, SERIES 5 | JANUARY 12, 2013 | BOSCO NG | BRENT FRIEDMAN |

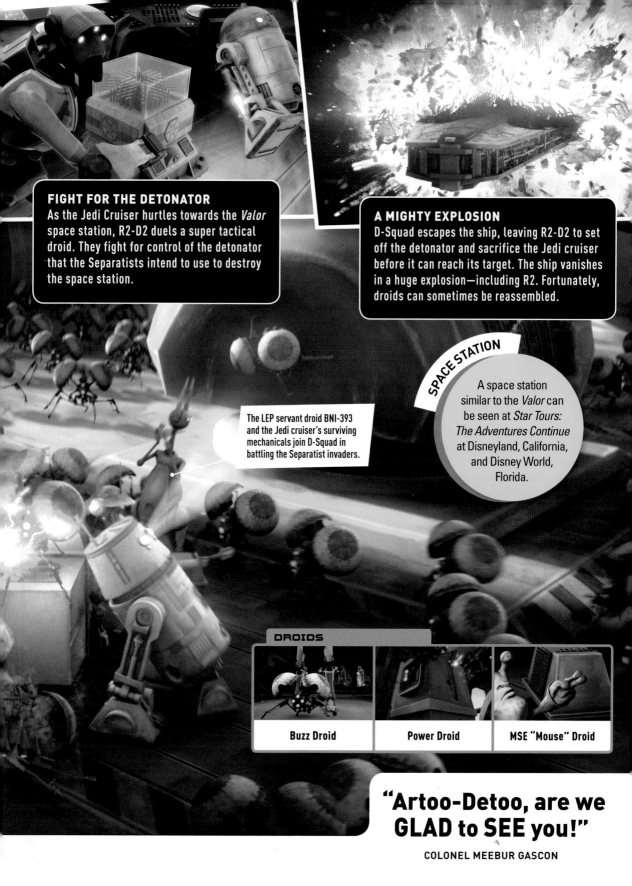

## FIGHT FOR THE DETONATOR

As the Jedi Cruiser hurtles towards the *Valor* space station, R2-D2 duels a super tactical droid. They fight for control of the detonator that the Separatists intend to use to destroy the space station.

## A MIGHTY EXPLOSION

D-Squad escapes the ship, leaving R2-D2 to set off the detonator and sacrifice the Jedi cruiser before it can reach its target. The ship vanishes in a huge explosion—including R2. Fortunately, droids can sometimes be reassembled.

### SPACE STATION

A space station similar to the *Valor* can be seen at *Star Tours: The Adventures Continue* at Disneyland, California, and Disney World, Florida.

The LEP servant droid BNI-393 and the Jedi cruiser's surviving mechanicals join D-Squad in battling the Separatist invaders.

### DROIDS

| Buzz Droid | Power Droid | MSE "Mouse" Droid |
| --- | --- | --- |

## "Artoo-Detoo, are we GLAD to SEE you!"

COLONEL MEEBUR GASCON

## DARTH MAUL AND Savage

Opress travel to the planet Florrum, where they intimidate some of Hondo Ohnaka's pirates into helping them build a new criminal organization to rival Hondo's. Obi-Wan and Adi Gallia follow the two Sith brothers, setting the stage for a deadly duel between Jedi and Sith.

### A CRUEL BLOW

Arriving on Florrum, Maul and Savage convince some of Hondo's pirates to join them and attack Hondo's base there. Obi-Wan and Adi intervene, but Savage beats Adi in a duel and strikes her down.

The Sith stole their cargo ship from the space station above Cybloc.

## REVIVAL

### "STRENGTH IN CHARACTER CAN DEFEAT STRENGTH IN NUMBERS."

**DROID**

**Spaceport Police Droid**

**LOCATION**

**Cybloc Transfer Station**

**#101**
EPISODE 1, SERIES 5

**AIRDATE**
SEPTEMBER 29, 2012

**DIRECTOR**
STEWARD LEE

**WRITER**
CHRIS COLLINS

## TWO AGAINST ONE

While Hondo battles the rebel pirates, Obi-Wan engages the two Sith, wielding Adi's lightsaber as well as his own. He cuts off Savage's arm, and the brothers flee.

## HONDO AND PIRATES

Maul and Savage race for their ship, but find an unexpected obstacle in their path: Hondo's pirates have reunited and are now all attacking the Sith.

### NOTABLE CHARACTERS

**Darth Maul**

**Obi-Wan Kenobi**

**Savage Opress**

The Sith use their Force powers to dominate the weak-minded. But Hondo's pirates have another weakness: a bottomless greed for credits.

### PRIZED OUTFIT

The Snivvian who talks to Obi-Wan and Adi in this episode wears the same outfit as the 1970s "Blue Snaggletooth" action figure available through the Sears catalog and now prized by collectors.

## "We are TWO, and you are NO MATCH for us both."

DARTH MAUL

**DARTH MAUL** and Savage Opress are floating above the planet Florrum in an escape pod when they are found and saved by Pre Vizsla's Death Watch. Vizsla hopes to use the two Sith in his plan to reconquer Mandalore. Maul has ideas of his own: He plans to create an underworld army of Black Sun soldiers, Pyke spice dealers, Hutt thugs, and Death Watch commandos.

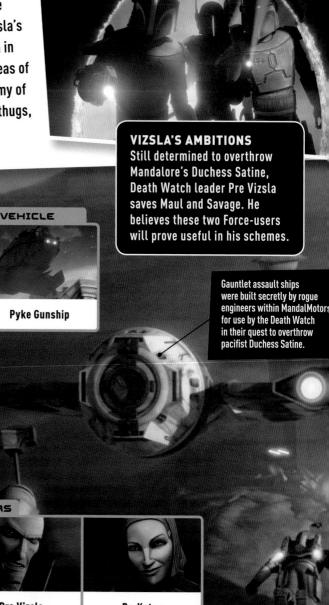

### VIZSLA'S AMBITIONS
Still determined to overthrow Mandalore's Duchess Satine, Death Watch leader Pre Vizsla saves Maul and Savage. He believes these two Force-users will prove useful in his schemes.

Gauntlet assault ships were built secretly by rogue engineers within MandalMotors for use by the Death Watch in their quest to overthrow pacifist Duchess Satine.

# EMINENCE

## "ONE VISION CAN HAVE MANY INTERPRETATIONS."

**DROID**

Chiewab Medical Droid

**VEHICLE**

Pyke Gunship

**NOTABLE CHARACTERS**

| | | |
|---|---|---|
| Darth Maul | Pre Vizsla | Bo-Katan |
| Jabba the Hutt | Ziton Moj | Lom |

**LOCATION**

Zanbar

| #102 EPISODE 14, SEASON 5 | AIRDATE JANUARY 19, 2013 | DIRECTOR KYLE DUNLEVY | WRITER CHRIS COLLINS |

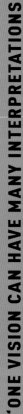

## BUILDING AN EMPIRE
Maul and Vizsla take over a Black Sun crime ring and attract Pyke spice dealers to their cause. They try to recruit the Hutts, but the Hutts' gangsters attack their forces with hired thugs. Bo-Katan and her airborne unit, the Nite Owls, race to the rescue.

## TAKE ME TO YOUR LEADER
With the Nite Owls' help, Maul and Savage defeat the Hutts' hired bounty hunters. But a final confrontation awaits with the crime lord Jabba the Hutt in his palace on Tatooine.

### SITH SALVAGE
The scene in this episode in which Death Watch enters the escape pod is an homage to the 1986 classic science-fiction movie *Aliens*.

Jabba's palace sits on the edge of the Dune Sea. It was originally a monastery built by the mysterious religious order of B'omarr Monks.

### OLD ADVERSARIES
The Black Sun criminal organization was developed for 1996's *Shadows of the Empire* novel and comics.

## "Our combined strength WILL be rewarded."
DARTH MAUL

**HAVING GATHERED HIS** army, Darth Maul plots the invasion of Mandalore. His thugs will attack the planet and sow chaos; then Death Watch will swoop in to win the people's allegiance by seeming to defeat the criminals. Pre Vizsla agrees to Maul's strategy. He intends to betray the Sith, however, once Maul has overthrown Satine, and then take over Mandalore himself.

### ATTACK AT PEACE PARK
Black Sun criminals storm Mandalore's Peace Park, spreading terror. As similar attacks occur across Mandalore, Death Watch warriors descend to capture the thugs.

Mandalore's warrior codes force Vizsla to accept Maul's challenge. But there's no rule about fighting fair, so he attacks the Sith with every weapon he has.

**SHADES OF REASON**

"ALLIANCES CAN STALL TRUE INTENTIONS."

## NOTABLE CHARACTERS

Darth Maul

Pre Vizsla

Bo-Katan

Duchess Satine Kryze

Prime Minister Almec

**#103**
EPISODE 15, SEASON 5

**AIRDATE**
JANUARY 26, 2013

**DIRECTOR**
BOSCO NG

**WRITER**
CHRIS COLLINS

214

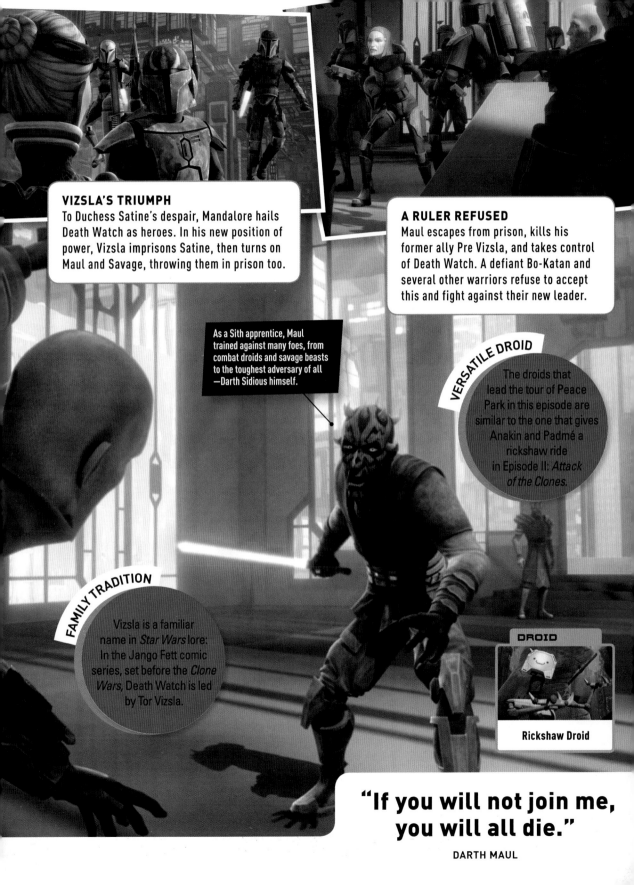

**VIZSLA'S TRIUMPH**
To Duchess Satine's despair, Mandalore hails
Death Watch as heroes. In his new position of
power, Vizsla imprisons Satine, then turns on
Maul and Savage, throwing them in prison too.

**A RULER REFUSED**
Maul escapes from prison, kills his
former ally Pre Vizsla, and takes control
of Death Watch. A defiant Bo-Katan and
several other warriors refuse to accept
this and fight against their new leader.

As a Sith apprentice, Maul
trained against many foes, from
combat droids and savage beasts
to the toughest adversary of all
—Darth Sidious himself.

**VERSATILE DROID**
The droids that
lead the tour of Peace
Park in this episode are
similar to the one that gives
Anakin and Padmé a
rickshaw ride
in Episode II: *Attack
of the Clones.*

**FAMILY TRADITION**
Vizsla is a familiar
name in *Star Wars* lore:
In the Jango Fett comic
series, set before the *Clone
Wars*, Death Watch is led
by Tor Vizsla.

**DROID**

**Rickshaw Droid**

# "If you will not join me, you will all die."

DARTH MAUL

**DARTH MAUL SITS** on the throne of Mandalore, apparently victorious. He has one remaining goal: to take revenge on his old foe, Obi-Wan Kenobi. While Maul uses Duchess Satine to draw Obi-Wan into a trap, Bo-Katan Kryze and her Nite Owls fight against Maul for Mandalore's freedom—and Darth Sidious decides it is time to confront his former apprentice.

### A CRY FOR HELP
Bo-Katan and her allies spring Satine from prison. The Duchess contacts Obi-Wan, unaware that this is what Maul wants. Once she has sent her message, Satine is recaptured by Death Watch.

### DARTH DEBUT
This episode marks the first appearance of Darth Sidious in the flesh. In all previous episodes, he appears only as a hologram.

Sidious can appear frail and slow, but the Sith Lord should not be underestimated—he is a master of all forms of lightsaber combat.

## THE LAWLESS

"MORALITY SEPARATES HEROES FROM VILLAINS."

### NOTABLE CHARACTERS

| | | |
|---|---|---|
| Darth Maul | Savage Opress | Darth Sidious |
| Obi-Wan Kenobi | Duchess Satine Kryze | Bo-Katan Kryze |

**#104**
EPISODE 16, SEASON 5

**AIRDATE**
FEBRUARY 2, 2013

**DIRECTOR**
BRIAN KALIN O'CONNELL

**WRITER**
CHRIS COLLINS

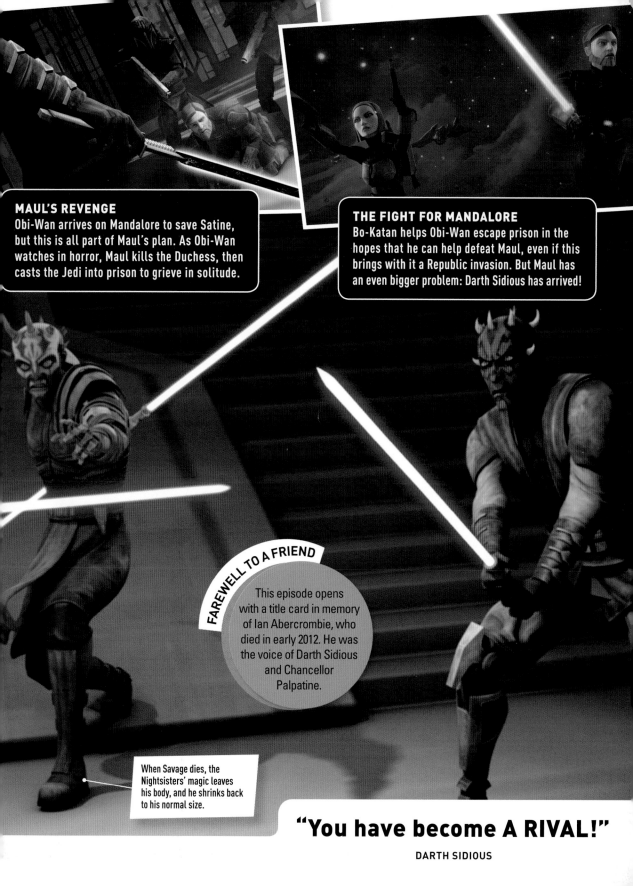

**MAUL'S REVENGE**
Obi-Wan arrives on Mandalore to save Satine, but this is all part of Maul's plan. As Obi-Wan watches in horror, Maul kills the Duchess, then casts the Jedi into prison to grieve in solitude.

**THE FIGHT FOR MANDALORE**
Bo-Katan helps Obi-Wan escape prison in the hopes that he can help defeat Maul, even if this brings with it a Republic invasion. But Maul has an even bigger problem: Darth Sidious has arrived!

**FAREWELL TO A FRIEND**
This episode opens with a title card in memory of Ian Abercrombie, who died in early 2012. He was the voice of Darth Sidious and Chancellor Palpatine.

When Savage dies, the Nightsisters' magic leaves his body, and he shrinks back to his normal size.

**"You have become A RIVAL!"**
DARTH SIDIOUS

**ANAKIN AND AHSOKA** are summoned to Coruscant to investigate a bombing in the Jedi Temple amid whisperings that a Jedi may have been responsible. Surrounded by rising distrust and paranoia, they begin by looking for clues at the bomb site. Their investigations uncover a sinister explanation which does not take them very far outside the Jedi Temple.

## HUNTING FOR CLUES

Anakin and Ahsoka search for clues with analysis droid Russo-ISC. A maintenance worker named Jackar Bowmani was in the right place at the right time to be the bomber—and he is missing.

# SABOTAGE

## "SOMETIMES EVEN THE SMALLEST DOUBT CAN SHAKE THE GREATEST BELIEF."

Jedi can use the Force to detect strong emotions or impressions. But the emotional shock of the bombing is so intense that it blots out everything else.

### HITCH HOMAGE

This episode is the first in a four-part story arc. Each of the episode names is taken from a classic movie by legendary director Alfred Hitchcock.

**#105**
EPISODE 17, SEASON 5

**AIRDATE**
FEBRUARY 9, 2013

**DIRECTOR**
BRIAN KALIN
O'CONNELL

**WRITER**
CHARLES MURRAY

## MEET THE WIDOW
Protestors at the Jedi Temple blame the Jedi for the violence of the war. One approaches Anakin: It is Jackar's widow, Letta Turmond, who appears desperate to find her husband.

## EXPLOSIVE EVIDENCE
Russo-ISC discovers disturbing evidence that shows Jackar himself was the bomb. Confronted by Anakin and Ahsoka, Letta admits feeding Jackar deadly nano-droids, which made him explode. But was Letta really working alone?

Through painstaking work, Russo-ISC and his analysis droids have recreated the trajectory and original position of each piece of bomb debris.

### CSI CORUSCANT
Russo-ISC's name and mannerisms are a nod to David Caruso's character, Horatio Caine, on the television show *CSI: Miami*.

### DROIDS

**Analysis Droid**

**Nano-Droid**

### NOTABLE CHARACTERS

**Anakin Skywalker**

**Ahsoka Tano**

### VEHICLES

**Jedi Interceptor**

**Russo-ISC**

**Letta Turmond**

# "There are going to be Jedi who disappoint us, Ahsoka."
ANAKIN SKYWALKER

**LETTA TURMOND** is in custody at a Republic base for her role in bombing the Jedi Temple. Ahsoka visits her, only to watch in horror as an unseen killer strangles her with the Force. When Ahsoka is imprisoned for Letta's murder, a mysterious benefactor appears to help her—but each bit of help just makes Ahsoka look more guilty.

## LETTA'S LAST WORDS
Letta tells Ahsoka that a Jedi masterminded the bombing, but she is silenced when an unknown assailant strangles her. On the security feed it looks like Ahsoka was Letta's killer.

### LOCATION
**Republic Base**

# THE JEDI WHO KNEW TOO MUCH

## "COURAGE BEGINS BY TRUSTING ONESELF."

**A LONG DROP**
The confrontation between Anakin and Ahsoka in the pipe is an homage to the well-known scene in the 1993 movie *The Fugitive*.

**#106**
EPISODE 18, SEASON 5

**AIRDATE**
FEBRUARY 16, 2013

**DIRECTOR**
DANNY KELLER

**WRITER**
CHARLES MURRA[...]

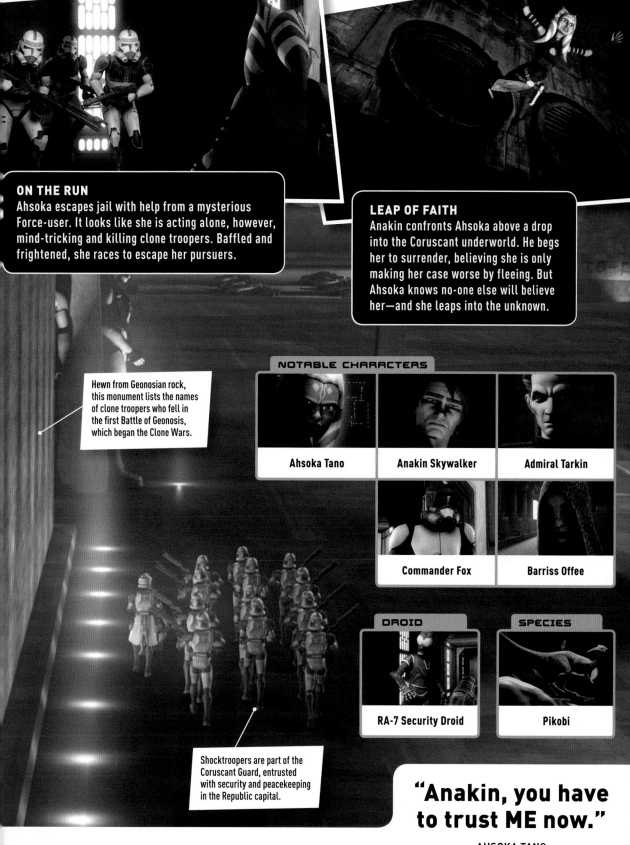

## ON THE RUN
Ahsoka escapes jail with help from a mysterious Force-user. It looks like she is acting alone, however, mind-tricking and killing clone troopers. Baffled and frightened, she races to escape her pursuers.

## LEAP OF FAITH
Anakin confronts Ahsoka above a drop into the Coruscant underworld. He begs her to surrender, believing she is only making her case worse by fleeing. But Ahsoka knows no-one else will believe her—and she leaps into the unknown.

Hewn from Geonosian rock, this monument lists the names of clone troopers who fell in the first Battle of Geonosis, which began the Clone Wars.

## NOTABLE CHARACTERS

**Ahsoka Tano**

**Anakin Skywalker**

**Admiral Tarkin**

**Commander Fox**

**Barriss Offee**

## DROID

**RA-7 Security Droid**

## SPECIES

**Pikobi**

Shocktroopers are part of the Coruscant Guard, entrusted with security and peacekeeping in the Republic capital.

## "Anakin, you have to trust ME now."
AHSOKA TANO

**AHSOKA FLEES INTO** Coruscant's underlevels and forms an unlikely alliance with Asajj Ventress, who is now working as a bounty hunter. Ahsoka gets a tip from Barriss Offee that could prove her innocence: Letta Turmond visited an old munitions warehouse in the underlevels. Yet when Ahsoka investigates the warehouse, someone is waiting for her.

## RELUCTANT ALLIES

Ventress agrees to help Ahsoka in return for the promise of a pardon for her crimes. They are spotted by clones, but escape. After they part ways, someone attacks Asajj, stealing her mask and sabers.

## HERE, KITTY

The tooka, also known as an Adoris feline, was first seen as Numa's doll in the episode "Innocents of Ryloth."

Coruscant's surface is divided into levels, from the lightless, uninhabited Level 1 to lofty, wealthy Level 5127. Asajj and Ahsoka fight the clones on Level 1312.

# TO CATCH A JEDI

## "NEVER BECOME DESPERATE ENOUGH TO TRUST THE UNTRUSTWORTHY."

**VEHICLE**

**Police Gunship**

**DROID**

**Underworld Police**

**SPECIES**

**Tooka**

**#107**
EPISODE 19, SEASON 5

**AIRDATE**
FEBRUARY 23, 2013

**DIRECTOR**
KYLE DUNLEVY

**WRITER**
CHARLES MURRAY

## UNDERWORLD BATTLE
Exploring the old warehouse, Ahsoka finds evidence of nano-droids—and is attacked by someone she thinks is Asajj. The mysterious figure defeats Ahsoka, then hides as clones storm the warehouse.

## PADAWAN CAPTURED
The clones stun Ahsoka, forcing a dismayed Anakin to confront the evidence: Ahsoka was seen with Asajj Ventress and captured in a warehouse full of nano-droids like those used in the Temple bombing. Is she a traitor?

Commander Wolffe's Wolf Pack squad conducts the hunt for Ahsoka alongside the shocktroopers of the Coruscant Guard.

## NOTABLE CHARACTERS

| Ahsoka Tano | Asajj Ventress | Anakin Skywalker | Commander Wolffe | Barriss Offee |
|---|---|---|---|---|

# "These are strange times."
ASAJJ VENTRESS

**THE JEDI ORDER** expels Ahsoka, believing her guilty of the Temple bombing. She is arrested and will stand trial for treason against the Republic. Anakin searches the lower levels of Coruscant for Asajj Ventress, convinced that she is really behind the attacks. The evidence he finds leads him back to the Jedi Temple—and a showdown with the real traitor.

### TRACKING A DARK JEDI
Anakin hunts down Ventress, who convinces him that the attacks are not her work, giving him a valuable clue: to look again at Barriss Offee's role in the sinister events.

## THE WRONG JEDI

### "NEVER GIVE UP HOPE, NO MATTER HOW DARK THINGS SEEM."

**DARK FORTRESS**
The lights and cylindrical terminals of the military courtroom in this episode foreshadow the architecture of the Death Star.

Jedi Master Luminara Unduli and Tutso Mara taught Barriss to fight most effectively with a lightsaber. But she is no match for the Chosen One.

**MYSTERY UNREVEALED**
Anakin interrupts the tribunal to reveal the truth about Ahsoka's innocence before Palpatine reads the verdict. Would Ahsoka have been found guilty or innocent? We may never know.

**LOCATION**

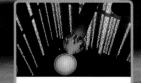

**Courtroom on Coruscant**

| #108 EPISODE 20, SEASON 5 | AIRDATE MARCH 2, 2013 | DIRECTOR DAVE FILONI | WRITER CHARLES MURRAY |
|---|---|---|---|

## ON TRIAL FOR TREASON
While Anakin tries to clear her name, Ahsoka faces a tribunal. Padmé defends her, with Admiral Tarkin as prosecutor. Not only is Ahsoka's freedom at stake, but her life as well.

## FATEFUL DECISION
After Anakin tricks Barriss into revealing that she is the traitor, Ahsoka is freed and welcomed back to the Jedi ranks. To Anakin's shock, she refuses to return. She chooses a new path.

### NOTABLE CHARACTERS

Ahsoka Tano

Anakin Skywalker

Barriss Offee

Chancellor Palpatine

Padmé Amidala

Admiral Tarkin

## "I've learned that trust is overrated."

BARRISS OFFEE

"The COUNCIL didn't trust me, so how can I TRUST myself?"

AHSOKA TANO

LONDON, NEW YORK, MUNICH,
MELBOURNE, and DELHI

**Editor** Pamela Afram
**Senior Editor** Elizabeth Dowsett
**Designer** Toby Truphet
**Pre-Production Producer** Rebecca Fallowfield
**Producer** Charlotte Oliver
**Managing Editor** Laura Gilbert
**Design Manager** Maxine Pedliham
**Publishing Manager** Julie Ferris
**Art Director** Ron Stobbart
**Publishing Director** Simon Beecroft

For Lucasfilm
**Executive Editor** J.W. Rinzler
**Keeper of the Holocron** Leland Chee
**Art Director** Troy Alders
**Director of Publishing** Carol Roeder

First published in the United States in 2013
by DK Publishing,
375 Hudson Street,
New York, New York 10014.
10 9 8 7 6 5 4 3 2 1
001–187422–June/13

Page design copyright © 2013
Dorling Kindersley Limited.

Published in Great Britain by Dorling Kindersley Limited.

A CIP catalog record for this book is available from the
Library of Congress.

ISBN: 978-1-4654-0873-0

Color reproduction by Alta Image in the UK.
Printed and bound in China by South China.

DK would like to thank Nicola Hodgson and Zoë Hedges
for editorial work, Laura Nickoll for proofreading, and
Lisa Lanzarini, Mark Richards, and Clive Savage for
design work.

Discover more at:
www.dk.com

Visit the official Star Wars site:
www.starwars.com

**ACKNOWLEDGMENTS**